WITHDRAWN

D1238532

Morton's
The
Cookbook

CONTENTS

WILLIE RANDOLPH'S FAVORITE: CRAB CAKE "BLT" SANDWICH

INTRODUCTION

Since the first Morton's opened in Chicago in 1978, we have been featuring USDA prime aged beef with "all the trimmings." Consistent quality is the name of the game for us, and it's my job to make sure we offer it in all of our more than eighty Morton's in the United States and abroad. We take great pride in knowing that Morton's The Steakhouse restaurants are the real deal. It's not surprising that Morton's is the most recognized fine-dining brand in the world—something that makes us extremely happy.

This means that when you dine at Morton's you know you will savor juicy, thick steaks cooked to perfection, accompanied by any number of delicious appetizers, soups, salads, and side dishes, and followed by indulgent desserts. We make the best cocktails in town, and our wine cellar is unrivaled. Without a doubt, when you visit Morton's The Steakhouse, you are in for a special treat!

And in *Morton's The Cookbook*, we share many of the recipes and secrets that make a dinner at Morton's so special. Our guests love to dine with us because not only do they know to expect great service and a warm, friendly atmosphere, but the food will be perfectly cooked with flavors that burst with freshness and, yes, familiarity. This is why our recipes translate so well to the home kitchen. Nothing is too exotic or out of the ordinary and yet everything is downright delicious and always approachable.

To start, you might select a Heavenly Cosmopolitan or a glass of full-bodied red wine. Follow your cocktail with Tuna Tartare or New York Strip Steak and Beefsteak Tomato Salad, a Morton's Center-Cut Iceberg Salad and perhaps a steaming bowl of Morton's Five-Onion Soup, a glorious marriage of sweet onions, rich beef broth, and melted cheese. For a main course, you might decide to have the Bone-in Ribeye or Morton's New York Strip Steak. To accompany the main course, many choose our Sautéed Garlic Green Beans, which are truly addictive, and our sinfully rich and creamy Macaroni and Cheese. To end the meal, you might try our

Double Chocolate Mousse or Honey-Glazed Apple Pastry. Or instead of a traditional dessert, you might be happier with one of our dessert cocktails, such as our Pistachio Mochatini. Who wouldn't leave on cloud nine, totally satisfied, and already dreaming of the next visit?

And as you will discover on the following pages, Morton's is more than just great steaks. We have great sandwiches, soups and salads, enticing appetizers, fish and seafood dishes to satisfy the most discriminating fish lover, lamb and poultry, and side dishes to please everyone.

When we decided to write a second cookbook, we wanted to bring our recipes into your home kitchen as successfully as we had in our first book, *Morton's Steak Bible.* We looked beyond our menu to the people who make up our organization. We also eyed the many locations where we have Morton's steakhouses, from Chicago to Palm Beach, New York to Los Angeles, Seattle to Honolulu, Vancouver to Singapore. While the menus at the restaurants in these and all our restaurants are exactly like the menus in every other Morton's, the geography, local foods, and local kitchen talent dictate some of the flavors of the food served all over the world.

With all this in mind, I decided to create a cookbook with recipes that reflect the spirit of Morton's, even if not every single one of them appears on our menu exactly as presented here. Some of the dishes in the book are on our menu, some are made exclusively for private parties or staff meals, and others are my own creations or those of our Morton's family. All in all, it is truly a winning collection, perfect for re-creating the great flavors of a Morton's steakhouse at home.

OUR STEAKS

Morton's is known for "The Best Steaks Anywhere." We feature USDA prime aged beef, which in and of itself is a feat, since prime beef comprises less than 2 percent of all the beef produced in the country. To find our meat, we still rely on the same two Chicago beef purveyors we have partnered with for three decades. In the early days, Jimmy the Butcher cut our steaks in a back room of the restaurant, but as we grew, this was not practical and so we took Jimmy's dictates to the suppliers. To this day, these suppliers hand cut the meat for us, following Jimmy's specifications. We let the meat age for three to four weeks to ensure it is as tender and flavorful as can be. All our steaks, chops, and roasts come to us this way.

We take the meat from our large coolers 30 to 60 minutes before cooking to get rid of the chill. Letting the chill subside is an important step and one the home cook should heed. Never put a cold steak on the grill or a cold roast in the oven. When it's allowed to come to a very cool room temperature, it cooks more evenly. With larger cuts, such as roasts, it is more critical than ever if you want perfectly cooked meat. The cooking times throughout the book are based on meat that has already reached room temperature (or "cool" room temperature, to be more accurate). The only exception to this rule is chopped meat. This should be refrigerated until it's time to cook it.

A meat's grade is determined by the marbling, the weblike structure of fat content running through the muscle. The finer, more even, and generous the marbling, the higher the grade of the beef. As mentioned above, for the most part, consumers can't get prime beef but this should not deter you. High-end choice beef can be quite good.

If you do see USDA prime beef in the market, grab it. Despite its high price, you won't be disappointed. Yet chances are you will have to be content with high-end choice beef, which is the next best thing and so there is no reason for regret. When you ask the butcher to cut steaks for you, whether you are buying prime or choice, ask for center cuts. These tend to be the most tender and are less apt to have tough veins.

My first recommendation is to buy beef and other meat from a butcher you know. He will cut steaks and chops to your specifications and he can steer you in the direction of what is best in his meat case. If you don't have a butcher nearby, order beef from a reputable catalog or online service. This can be more costly, but there are some very good websites that sell premium products, so when you plan a special meal, you won't be sorry. If you end up at the supermarket, ask the butcher behind the glass window near the meat counter to cut the meat for you rather than buying it from the packaged meat case. You might be surprised how helpful these folks are and if you are lucky, you will establish a relationship with one or two of these people. This way, you'll always be well cared for.

When you buy beef, examine it for marbling. This is fat, but don't be put off. It's the fat that gives the beef its amazing flavor. Beef should be true red with creamy flecks of fat running through it. Big ropes of fat are not desirable; it should be thin and webbed. As an exception, ribeye steaks often have a natural thick kernel (or deposit) of fat. Avoid beef that is very bright red, browning, or two-toned; has yellowish fat; or is either under-marbled or packed with thick knobs of fat. Beef should be capped with a thick coat of cream-colored fat—the fat you see on the rim of the steak. Fat adds flavor, texture, and juiciness.

MORTON'S CHAMPAGNE COCKTAIL

COCKTAILS

ICED VODKA WITH SIRLOIN GARNISH

—

HEAVENLY COSMOPOLITAN

—

HEAVENLY PEAR MORTINI

—

KEY LIME MARGARITA

—

CAIPIRINHA

—

SAZERAC

—

AMERICANO COCKTAIL

—

POMEGRANATE-SAKE COCKTAIL

—

MORTON'S BLOODY MARY

—

PORT SANGRIA

—

MORTON'S CHAMPAGNE COCKTAIL

—

MORTON'S VODKA COCKTAIL

—

WILD DAISY

—

SPICY PEAR LEMONADE

—

GUAVA CAIPIRISSIMA

—

KENTUCKY DERBY MINT JULEP

—

COOL AS A CUCUMBER

CALLOWAY COUNTY PUBLIC LIBRARY

ICED VODKA
WITH SIRLOIN GARNISH

We think vodka is just the thing to drink with steak and we especially like it with steak tartare. The icy cold vodka never masks the flavor of the seasoned meat and cuts through the fat like a sleek knife. And yes! This cocktail is garnished with a tiny piece of raw beef. Perfect! **SERVES 4 TO 6**

One 375-ml bottle Ketel One vodka
4 to 6 thin 2-inch-long slices prime or choice
sirloin beef (see Note)

2 to 3 teaspoons cream cheese, at room
temperature
Celery salt

Put the vodka bottle in a clean, opened cardboard pint container, the kind that comes filled with cream or half-and-half. Pour water into the container to come nearly to the top of the container and about two-thirds of the way up the bottle. Freeze the bottle in the carton for at least 1½ hour or until the water freezes solid.

Lay the pieces of sirloin on a work surface and spread the cream cheese over them. Season each one with a sprinkle of celery salt. Roll each slice of meat into a cylinder and secure with a decorative plastic or wooden pick.

Peel the cardboard from the ice.

Put the meat garnish in four to six 4-ounce shot glasses and pour some vodka over it. Serve.

NOTE: You can drop flowers, spices, or berries—almost anything really—into the water before freezing for a decorative presentation and then put the frozen cube of ice with the vodka in the center of the table and let everyone serve themselves.

The sirloin is easy to slice from a partially frozen piece of meat. Plan ahead and put some steak in the freezer about an hour before you want to make the cocktail.

HEAVENLY COSMOPOLITAN

If "the girls" from Sex and the City *had tasted our version of a Cosmo topped with light-as-air foam, they never would have ended their HBO show!* **SERVES 1**

2 ounces Ketel One Citroen vodka

¼ cup cranberry juice

½ ounce Grand Marnier

Juice of ¼ lime (2 generous lime wedges)

2 ounces Heavenly Foam, page 16

Pour the vodka, cranberry juice, Grand Marnier, and lime juice into a cocktail shaker filled with ice cubes. Shake 15 times. Strain into a martini glass.

Top with the foam and serve immediately.

✍ CELEBRITY CLIP ✍

DURING AND SINCE the six-year run of HBO's *Sex and the City* we have spotted most of its leading actors at Morton's The Steakhouse. We recently hosted Kristin Davis, who played Charlotte on the show and in the movie, at our San Francisco Morton's. Jason Lewis, who was Smith Jerrod in both the show and the film, dined at our Burbank, California, location, while Mr. Big himself, Chris Noth, occupied a table at the Morton's in Manhattan at Forty-fifth Street and Fifth Avenue. To cap it off, the *Plain Dealer*, Cleveland's major daily newspaper, surmised that if Cynthia Nixon, who played Miranda, were to move to Cleveland, she would no doubt frequent the "art deco bar" that is known as Morton's Bar 12•21, at our Morton's The Steakhouse located in Cleveland's downtown Tower City Center. ✍

HEAVENLY PEAR MORTINI

When we top one of our famous Mortinis with foam, it becomes more of a treat than ever. Your guests will be charmed; it's worth the extra effort. **SERVES 1**

2 ounces Absolut Pears vodka
2 tablespoons pear purée, see Note
1 ounce limoncello liqueur

2 tablespoons sweet-and-sour mix, see Note
2 ounces Heavenly Foam, recipe follows

Pour the vodka, pear purée, limoncello, and sweet-and-sour mix into a cocktail shaker filled with ice cubes. Shake 15 times. Strain into a martini glass.

Top with the foam and serve immediately.

NOTE: We use frozen pear purée called Perfect Purée of Napa Valley. Be sure to defrost it before using. You can order it online at www.perfectpuree.com, or make your own pear purée using peeled ripe pears and processing them in a food processor.

We use Daily's Bar Sour Mix, which is sold at supermarkets across the country.

HEAVENLY FOAM

You need a whip canister to make foam, charged with an N2O cream charger. These are sold at gourmet shops and online from outlets such as Williams-Sonoma and Chefs Catalog. Don't let the idea of another piece of kitchen equipment put you off. They are easy to use and don't take up much room. The trick is to chill them once filled for at least 1 hour. **MAKES ENOUGH FOAM FOR 5 TO 6 DRINKS**

½ cup egg whites (3 to 4 large egg whites)
½ cup passion fruit purée

½ cup sweet-and-sour mix, see Note
2 ounces Grand Marnier

Put the egg whites, passion fruit purée, sweet-and-sour mix, and Grand Marnier into a chilled iSi Gourmet Whip or Cream Whipper canister, or similar foamer. Refrigerate for at least 1 hour. Charge the foam canister with 1 or 2 N$_2$O cream chargers and shake 5 times. Use immediately.

NOTE: We use Daily's Bar Sour Mix, which is sold at supermarkets across the country.

KEY LIME MARGARITA

This twist on a classic margarita tastes great with any dish that is high in citrus, such as ceviche. The juice from Key limes is more concentrated than other lime juice, so if you are using a regular lime instead, you may need a little more juice. **SERVES 1**

2 Key limes

2 ounces Patrón Silver tequila

2 teaspoons agave nectar, see Note

Cut half of one of the limes into cubes. Cut the remaining half into wedges for garnish. Put the cubes in an empty cocktail shaker. With the back of a long-handled spoon or a cocktail muddler, press on the lime pieces to release their juice and the essential oils in the lime rind.

Add the tequila, nectar, and the juice of the remaining lime. Fill the shaker with ice cubes and shake 22 times. Strain into a martini glass and garnish with a wedge of lime dropped into the glass.

NOTE: Agave nectar, sometimes called agave syrup, is about 90 percent fructose. The agave plant grows in semiarid Mexico, where it is distilled into tequila. Agave nextar is sold in natural food stores such as Whole Foods and in some supermarkets and specialty shops.

CAIPIRINHA

This Brazilian cocktail is loaded with fresh lime juice and with a cane spirit called Leblon Cachaça. This is a refreshing drink, a great start to any meal. **SERVES 1**

½ lime, cut into 6 cubes

2 tablespoons Simple Syrup, recipe follows

2 ounces Leblon Cachaça

Sprig of fresh mint

Put the lime in an empty cocktail shaker and with the back of a long-handled spoon or a cocktail muddler, press on the lime pieces to release their juice and the essential oils in the lime rind. Add the syrup and Leblon Cachaça and muddle a few more times to blend the flavors.

Add crushed ice to fill the shaker and shake. Pour into a large collins glass and garnish with the mint sprig.

SIMPLE SYRUP

This sugar syrup is used as often in cocktails as in desserts. It's easy to make and keeps for weeks in the refrigerator. **MAKES ABOUT 1 CUP**

1 cup sugar

In a small, heavy saucepan, mix the sugar with 1 cup water. Bring to a boil over medium-high heat, stirring for about 1 minute, or until the sugar dissolves and the syrup is clear.

Remove the pan from the heat and let the syrup cool to room temperature. Transfer to a glass jar with a tight-fitting lid and refrigerate. The syrup can be refrigerated for up to 1 month.

SAZERAC

This New Orleans traditional cocktail is made with smoky rye whiskey, which means it stands up to spicy, full-flavored foods such as those so beloved in the Crescent City. Peychaud's bitters are the bitters of choice for New Orleans and make the cocktail authentic, but if you have Angostura bitters on hand, they work, too. You only need a tiny bit of the anise-flavored absinthe. (Absinthe is once again legal in the United States. It had been banned in 1912 because of the chemical thujone it contains in small amounts. Some absinthe is legal again when it is labeled as being "thujone-free," which means it has less than 10 parts-per-million thujone.) **SERVES 1**

3 ounces rye whiskey

2 tablespoons plus 1 teaspoon Simple Syrup, page 18

3 drops of Peychaud's bitters

1 large egg white, lightly whisked

Absinthe

1 lemon twist

Pour the whiskey, syrup, and bitters into a cocktail shaker and stir to mix. Fill the shaker with ice and add half of the egg white (discard the remaining egg white or use it for a second Sazerac). Shake 5 times.

Pour a small amount of absinthe into a tall collins glass. You need only enough to cover the bottom of the glass. Roll the absinthe in the glass to coat the sides and then pour out the remaining absinthe. The absinthe is only meant to season the glass.

Strain the whiskey mixture into the glass and garnish with the lemon twist.

AMERICANO COCKTAIL

Despite its name, this is a classic Italian cocktail, very similar to a Negroni. The botanicals in the gin are softened by the sweet vermouth, which makes this successful with spicy dishes. **SERVES 1**

1 ounce sweet vermouth

1 ounce Campari

Splash of club soda

1 round orange slice

Pour the vermouth and Campari into a cocktail shaker filled with ice. Shake very gently 2 to 3 times just to mix the ingredients.

   Strain the cocktail into a large highball glass filled with ice, add a splash of club soda to fill, and garnish with the orange slice.

POMEGRANATE-SAKE COCKTAIL

The slight sweetness of the pomegranate liqueur is balanced by the acidity of the sake. This makes this cocktail perfect with rich dishes and specifically with the Tempura Lobster Tail on page 188. **SERVES 1**

3 ounces sake

1 ounce Pama pomegranate liqueur

Pour the sake and liqueur into a cocktail shaker filled with ice. Shake 15 times.

   Strain into a martini glass.

POMEGRANATE-SAKE COCKTAIL

MORTON'S BLOODY MARY

Bloody Marys taste great with beef and, though we so often think of them as a brunch-only cocktail, are a terrific way to change up the evening. The heat and acidity are cut by the beef's protein and fat for a palate full of interesting flavors. **SERVES 1**

1 ounce Absolut Peppar vodka
⅓ cup Bloody Mary mix

GARNISHES
Gherkins wrapped in prosciutto
Anchovy-stuffed olives
Croutons wrapped with bacon
Celery stuffed with chive cream cheese
Mini bread and beef skewers
Asparagus and blue cheese skewers

Pour the vodka and Bloody Mary mix into a cocktail shaker filled with ice. Shake 15 times. Strain into a tall collins glass filled with ice. Garnish with the garnish of your choice.

PORT SANGRIA

Sangria made with port is a change from the usual wine punch and results in a deep, fruity drink that deliciously complements rich foods such as cheese—and in particular blue cheese. **SERVES 6 TO 7**

1 lemon, cut into 6 wedges and each wedge
    halved

1 orange, cut into 6 wedges and each wedge
    halved

1 lime, cut into 6 wedges and each wedge halved

1 peach, peeled and pitted, cut into 6 wedges
    and each wedge halved

1 knob of peeled fresh ginger,
    about 2 inches long

One 750-ml bottle ruby port

About 2 tablespoons ginger ale or club soda

6 to 7 round orange slices, for serving

In a large bowl, toss together the lemon, orange, lime, and peach pieces and the ginger. Pour the port over the fruit and ginger, cover, and refrigerate for at least 6 hours and up to 12 hours.

Strain the sangria into 6 to 7 tall collins glasses filled with ice. Top each glass with a splash of ginger ale. Garnish each glass with an orange slice and serve.

MORTON'S CHAMPAGNE COCKTAIL

Our champagne cocktail is a lovely, light refreshment made with pomegranate and orange liqueurs. We coat the rim of the glass with cinnamon sugar for an extra "zowie!" Everyone loves this. **SERVES 1**

1 orange wedge

1 to 2 teaspoons Cinnamon Sugar, recipe follows

2 drops of peach bitters, see Note

1 sugar cube

1 ounce Grand Marnier

1 tablespoon Pama pomegranate liqueur

Chilled Champagne or sparkling wine

Rub the orange wedge around the rim of a champagne flute to moisten it. Dip the rim in the cinnamon sugar to coat.

Drip the bitters on the sugar cube. Put the sugar cube in the bottom of the glass. Pour the Grand Marnier and pomegranate liqueur over the sugar cube. Fill the glass with the Champagne and serve right away.

NOTE: We use peach bitters made by Fee Brothers. It is easy to order online.

CINNAMON SUGAR

MAKES ¼ CUP

¼ cup sugar

1 teaspoon ground cinnamon

In a small bowl, stir the sugar and cinnamon together until well mixed. Transfer to a glass jar with a tight lid. The sugar will keep for several months.

MORTON'S VODKA COCKTAIL

What better to drink for brunch or lunch than a fruity cocktail with or without alcohol? Try a mango mint with or without vodka. Plan ahead to give the ice time to freeze. **SERVES 1**

Fresh mint leaves

2 ounces vodka

1 tablespoon mango nectar

Put a mint leaf in each cube of an ice cube tray. Fill with water and freeze.

Put 3 minted ice cubes in a highball glass and pour the vodka over the ice. Top with the mango nectar.

NOTE: For an alcohol-free mango mint, increase the amount of nectar poured over the ice cubes.

WILD DAISY

This herbaceous cocktail is terrific on spring and summer evenings for a light, refreshing drink and tastes great with steak, lamb, and chicken—just about any meat! It's also good with salads and small plates. If you don't want to make the lavender syrup, you can buy it from Monin Gourmet Syrups. **SERVES 1**

1 tablespoon dried lavender

½ cup Simple Syrup, page 18

2½-inches-long, peeled cucumber slice

2 ounces Sauza Hornitos Plata tequila

2 tablespoons fresh lime juice

1 fresh mint leaf

Put the lavender in the cooled syrup and refrigerate for about 8 hours to flavor the syrup. Strain the syrup after it chills.

Put the cucumber slice and 1 tablespoon of water in a cocktail shaker and with the back of a long-handled spoon or a cocktail muddler, press on the cucumber until pulpy. Strain through a fine-mesh sieve, pressing on the cucumber, to get 2 tablespoons of liquid.

Pour the tequila, lime juice, syrup, and cucumber water into a cocktail shaker. Shake 15 times. Pour into an old-fashioned glass filled with ice cubes and garnish with the mint.

SPICY PEAR LEMONADE

We have taken lemonade off the picnic table and put it on the cocktail menu. The Limoncello, sweet-and-sour mix, and ginger juice offer clear, dazzling flavors that evoke those of lemonade. **SERVES 1**

1½ ounces Absolut Pears vodka

½ ounce Limoncello liqueur

2 ounces fresh sweet-and-sour mix, see Note

Splash of ginger juice, such as Elixir G ginger
   Juice

Sparkling water

1 thin lemon slice

1 thin pear slice

In a highball glass, mix together the vodka, Limoncello, and sweet-and-sour mix. Add a splash of ginger juice and top with sparkling water.

Garnish the glass with the lemon and pear slices.

NOTE: We use Daily's Bar Sour Mix, which is sold at supermarkets across the country.

GUAVA CAIPIRISSIMA

This rum drink is bright and fruity. Once they discover it, our guests love it. **SERVES 1**

4 lime wedges, halved

2 tablespoons cubed fresh guava

½ ounce agave nectar

1½ ounces rum, see Note

1 ounce Cruzan guava-flavored rum

Put the lime wedges, guava, and agave nectar in a cocktail shaker and with the back of a long-handled spoon or a cocktail muddler, press on the fruit and muddle so that the lime wedges and guava are softened.

Add 1 cup of ice cubes and both rums. Shake vigorously and pour into a double old-fashioned glass. Do not strain.

NOTE: We use Cruzan Estate Diamond rum, which is a relatively light rum.

KENTUCKY DERBY MINT JULEP

Once a year, when the best Thoroughbreds in the world run for the roses, folks indulge in this refreshing cocktail. We love to make juleps on race day, but why not enjoy them any time of year? They are particularly good when the mint in your garden is fresh. Our guests order juleps to drink with thick, juicy steaks. **SERVES 1**

1 cup Simple Syrup, see page 18, see Note
9 sprigs fresh mint

2 ounces Kentucky bourbon, see Note

Put 8 mint sprigs in the cooled syrup and refrigerate for about 8 hours to flavor the syrup.

Fill a silver julep cup with crushed ice. Pour the bourbon and 1 tablespoon of the syrup over the ice. Stir rapidly with a spoon to frost the outside of the cup. Garnish with the remaining sprig of mint.

NOTE: You will not need all the syrup, unless you make more than one julep! We use Maker's Mark bourbon.

COOL AS A CUCUMBER

Cucumbers are naturally cool and refreshing, as is vodka, and so we thought this was a natural marriage. We were right. Try it with Warm Steak Salad on page 00 for a light meal—although it also goes down nicely with a simply grilled steak. **SERVES 1**

4 thin cucumber slices
2 tablespoons lime juice
1 ounce St. Germain elderflower liqueur

1½ ounces 100 proof vodka
Ginger beer

Put 3 slices of cucumber, lime juice, and elderflower liqueur in a cocktail shaker and with the back of a long-handled spoon or a cocktail muddler, press on the cucumber slices and muddle until mashed and well mixed with the lime juice and liqueur.

Add the vodka and then fill the shaker with ice. Shake vigorously and pour into a tall glass filled with ice. Top with a splash of ginger beer. Garnish with the remaining cucumber slice.

MORTON'S CENTER-CUT ICEBERG SALAD

APPETIZERS AND SALADS

SIRLOIN ROLLS

—

Leroy Neiman's Favorite
FIRST-COURSE LAMB CHOPS

—

SMOKED SALMON WEDGES

—

SIRLOIN STEAK TARTARE

—

TUNA TARTARE

—

TUNA SASHIMI BURGERS

—

OYSTERS ROCKEFELLER

—

STEAMED MUSSELS WITH GARLIC
AND TOMATO

—

TUNA CANAPÉS

—

KEY LIME MARINATED SEAFOOD

—

WARM BLUE-CHEESE DIP

—

MORTON'S CENTER-CUT ICEBERG
SALAD

—

Fran Drescher's Favorite
TOMATO, MOZZARELLA, AND
PROSCIUTTO SALAD

—

MIXED GREEN SALAD WITH
GRILLED SHRIMP

—

MAINE LOBSTER AND AVOCADO
SALAD

—

MORTON'S ASIAN SLAW

—

EDIE'S CHOPPED VEGETABLE SALAD

—

WARM STEAK SALAD WITH
ASIAN DRESSING

—

NEW YORK STRIP STEAK AND
BEEFSTEAK TOMATO SALAD

SIRLOIN ROLLS

The slightly elusive and yet unmistakable flavor of the lemongrass combined with the simple Asian-style sauce makes this appetizer hard to resist. It's great for parties or a treat for a few beef-loving friends gathered for a quick bite. It takes no time to cook and little effort to prepare. **SERVES 6**

¼ cup fish sauce

2 tablespoons sesame oil

2 tablespoons dry sherry

1 tablespoon minced shallot

1 tablespoon minced scallions, white
   and green parts

1 tablespoon minced peeled lemongrass

1 tablespoon soy sauce

1½ pounds partially frozen sirloin strip steak,
   fat trimmed, 2½ to 3 inches thick, see Note

6 lemongrass stalks, peeled and trimmed
   to ¼-inch diameter and cut into twelve
   6-inch pieces

1 tablespoon sugar

⅛ teaspoon cornstarch

2 tablespoons sunflower or canola oil

WINE RECOMMENDATION
With Asian-style dishes with lemongrass and fish sauce try a wine that accentuates the sweetness but that can stand up to the protein. The citrus in Sauvignon Blanc is perfect for this. We recommend The Crossings and Cloudy Bay, both from New Zealand.

For true indulgence you can't beat a late-harvest Riesling or Semillon. The sweetness and velvety texture of these wines are a treat and will balance the dish. We suggest Mer Soleil "Late" and Inniskillin.

In a small bowl, mix together the fish sauce, oil, sherry, shallot, scallion, lemongrass, and soy sauce until well blended. You will have about ¾ cup of chunky sauce. Divide the sauce approximately in half, each in a separate bowl. Set 1 bowl aside to use later.

Holding a knife at a sharp angle, slice the sirloin into 12 very thin slices, each 2½ to 3 inches wide. Lay the meat on a work surface and brush 1 side of each slice with sauce. Lay a lemongrass stalk lengthwise along each strip of meat and roll up. Arrange the rolls, seam sides down, in a shallow glass dish and brush the tops and sides with more sauce. You will, by now, have used all of 1 bowl of sauce. Cover and refrigerate the rolls for about 1 hour to give them time to absorb the flavors of the sauce and the lemongrass.

Whisk the sugar and cornstarch into the reserved sauce.

In a sauté pan large enough to hold the rolls, heat the oil over medium-high heat and when hot, cook the rolls, seam-side down, for about 1 minute or until browned. Use tongs to turn

recipe continues on page 36

the rolls very gently and continue to cook for another minute or so to brown on all sides. The meat is wrapped loosely around the lemongrass and so you will have to use great care.

Drizzle the reserved sauce over the rolls and cook for 3 to 4 minutes longer or until the sauce is heated through. Serve immediately.

NOTE: It's important that the steak be 2½ to 3 inches thick so that when it's sliced, the pieces will be wide and thin enough. Partially freezing the meat makes it easy to slice. Put the meat in the freezer about an hour before you will slice it.

↭ CELEBRITY CLIP ↭

MUSICIANS ON TOUR often stop into Morton's for a good steak or seafood dinner, appreciating the consistency from city to city. Recently, the Goo Goo Dolls stopped at nearly every Morton's The Steakhouse in the United States, sometimes visiting the same restaurant two consecutive nights, depending on their concert schedule. Lead signer Johnny Rzeznik apparently is a fan of our lobster tails and porterhouse steaks. Dave Matthews dined at the Morton's in Cleveland, Ohio, as did Adam Levine, lead singer for Maroon 5, who ducked into the Bar 12•21 there to watch a baseball playoff game and indulge in the Morton's Bar Bites menu. When in San Francisco, Billy Joel ordered our Chicago bone-in rib eye, a Caesar salad, and sautéed fresh spinach and mushrooms. The Pussy-Cat Dolls recently showed up for dinner at our new Morton's in Macau, located in the Venetian Resort Hotel and Casino. Celine Dion was seen there, as well.

Dolly Parton dined at the Morton's in downtown Atlanta, where she posed for photos with the staff, and the photos quickly found spots on our celebrity photo wall. Peter Frampton was a guest at our Beverly Hills location, which has long been a haven for top celebrities. Musical duo Elvis Costello and his wife, jazz singer Diana Krall, recently enjoyed the sesame-encrusted tuna and the New York strip at our Phoenix Morton's. Richard Marx and country music star Vince Gill showed up at our Nashville restaurant. When Richie Sambora and Jon Bon Jovi walked into our Toronto restaurant together, they caused quite a stir. Finally, American Idol's Randy Jackson seemed to think our prime aged beef made the grade when he dined at our Georgetown restaurant in Washington, D.C. ↭

FIRST-COURSE LAMB CHOPS

I loved the lamb chops I tasted in Hong Kong during my visit to our Morton's steakhouse there. They were from Tasmania and were as sweet and succulent as any I have ever had. At the restaurant, we use lamb from New Zealand and Australia, although American lamb is excellent, too. When you can find little lamb chops, try this simple and yet elegant starter. It's a sure winner. It's also LeRoy Neiman's favorite dish. His serigraphs adorn the walls of our Morton's steakhouses throughout the world. **SERVES 6**

12 petite lamb chops, each weighing
   about 2 ounces
Salt and freshly ground black pepper
1 tablespoon peanut oil

6 ounces Brie cheese, cut into 12 squares,
   each about 1½ inches square
2 tablespoons chopped fresh flat-leaf parsley,
   for serving

WINE RECOMMENDATION
The gaminess of lamb is most suited to a spicy wine. The Australians make the best wine for this pairing, which is not surprising considering there are more sheep than people Down Under. Try wines produced by Two Hands and Jacob's Creek.

COCKTAIL RECOMMENDATION
A single-malt scotch, such as a twelve-year-old Macallan, served over ice with a small amount of water.

Preheat the broiler.

Season the chops lightly with salt and pepper.

In a large sauté pan, heat the oil over high heat and when hot, cook the chops for 1 to 1½ minutes on each side, or just until rare.

Transfer the chops to a broiler pan and top each with a piece of cheese. Broil about 3 inches from the heat for about 45 seconds or until the cheese melts and starts to brown.

Serve garnished with the chopped parsley.

SMOKED SALMON WEDGES

This pizza is especially easy because you buy the pizza crust. We like Boboli, but you can substitute your favorite. If you are ambitious, make your own, but roll the dough out so that it's nice and thin. We suggest cutting this into small wedges for passing at parties, or larger pieces for a simple lunch or even a brunch dish. The fresh dill makes a big difference. It accentuates the salmon and makes everything taste divinely fresh. **MAKES ONE 12-INCH ROUND PIZZA; SERVES 6 TO 8**

One 12-inch thin-crust prepared pizza crust

¼ cup sour cream

2 tablespoons plus 2 teaspoons finely chopped red onion

2 tablespoons minced fresh dill

5 ounces smoked salmon, very thinly sliced

3 teaspoons drained capers

WINE RECOMMENDATION
Brut sparkling wine, such as Schramsberg or Krug, will fit very well. Dry Champagne is generally high in acid. For this reason, it is best paired with salty foods.

BEER RECOMMENDATION
Lager beer, such as Budweiser "Select" will go down perfectly. Beer and pizza . . . we all get that one.

Preheat the oven to 325°F. Position the oven rack in the center of the oven.

Put the crust directly on the oven rack and warm for about 5 minutes. Transfer the warm crust to a cutting board.

Spread the sour cream over the crust, leaving a ½-inch border. Sprinkle about half of the red onion over the sour cream and sprinkle half the dill over the onion.

Lay the salmon slices over the pizza to cover the sour cream, onion, and dill. Sprinkle the remaining onion and dill over the salmon and then scatter the capers over them. Cut the pizza into 12 wedges and serve at once.

SIRLOIN STEAK TARTARE

When we first opened Morton's in 1978, we listed steak tartare on the menu, much to the delight of our guests. Times change and it's no longer a Morton's menu item, although it remains one of my all-time favorites, and I still make it for guests in my home. When you make it, plan to serve it on the same day and always buy the absolute best beef you can find. Serve this with cocktail rye bread or toast points if you prefer something a little heartier than lettuce leaves.

SERVES 6 TO 8; MAKES ABOUT 2 ½ CUPS

3 anchovies, drained and finely chopped

½ cup finely chopped yellow onion

¼ cup egg yolks (from 3 to 4 large eggs)

1 tablespoon drained capers, finely chopped

2½ teaspoons ketchup

2½ teaspoons Dijon mustard

1½ teaspoons red wine vinegar

¾ teaspoon Worcestershire sauce

¾ teaspoon salt

½ teaspoon olive oil

½ teaspoon freshly ground white pepper

8 drops of Tabasco sauce or another hot pepper sauce

1 pound prime or choice sirloin, chopped, see Note

Romaine leaves, for serving

WINE RECOMMENDATION
American Pinot Noir tends to have higher alcohol and more woody characteristics than its French counterpart. Sonoma and Santa Barbara are great growing areas. The Pinot Noir will complement the mineral components of the beef and will also add nuance to the spiciness of the condiments. We recommend those produced by Sanford and Rochioli.

COCKTAIL RECOMMENDATION
Iced Vodka with Sirloin Garnish, page 12

In a mixing bowl, whisk together the anchovies, ¼ cup of the onion, the egg yolks, capers, ketchup, mustard, vinegar, Worcestershire sauce, salt, olive oil, and white pepper. Season with the hot pepper sauce.

Add the meat and using your hands, fold the meat into the mixed ingredients.

Line a serving platter with romaine lettuce leaves and spoon the beef tartare over the lettuce. Garnish with the remaining ¼ cup chopped onion and serve.

NOTE: When you make tartare, use the highest grade beef you can find. We suggest prime sirloin or Angus beef, which is a very high grade of choice meat. Do not buy it already chopped but instead ask the butcher to grind it for you. Tell the butcher you will be serving the meat raw and therefore he should take care that the grinder is clean so that there is no cross contamination with other kinds of meat. A good alternative is to grind the meat at home, using the meat grinder attachment for a standing mixer. A food processor will grind the meat too fine and should only be used with great caution.

TUNA TARTARE

Start with the best tuna you can buy—often labeled "sushi tuna"—and enjoy this delectable first course soon after making it. It's similar to but not exactly like tartare; it's chunkier and more fully marinated. The wonton chips are easy to fry and are perfect for serving with the tuna, although if you don't have time for them, you could substitute pita chips. **SERVES 4 TO 6**

3 cups sunflower or canola oil

24 wonton wrappers (3-inch square), sliced in half on the diagonal

1 pound best-quality tuna, cut into ½-inch dice

½ cup chopped scallions, white and green parts

1 clove fresh garlic, minced

1½ teaspoons toasted white sesame seeds, see Note

1 teaspoon crushed red pepper flakes

⅓ cup soy sauce

1 tablespoon sesame oil

WINE RECOMMENDATION
German Riesling (Kabinett) truly brings out the unctuous flavors of this mild fish. It will also temper the spiciness of the dish. You need to stay with a dry style. Try one by Joseph Prum.

COCKTAIL RECOMMENDATION
Caipirinha, page 18

In a heavy saucepan, heat the oil over medium heat until hot. The oil should register 350°F on a deep-fryer thermometer. When hot, fry 3 or 4 wonton wrappers for 20 to 30 seconds or until lightly golden. Lift from the hot oil with tongs and drain on paper towels. Continue frying until all 48 pieces are fried.

Put the chips in a basket or bowl, and keep uncovered until ready to use. If you need to store them longer than a few hours, you can put them in a tightly covered container for up to 24 hours.

In a small mixing bowl, stir together the tuna, scallions, garlic, sesame seeds, and red pepper flakes. Add the soy sauce and sesame oil and stir until incorporated.

Transfer the tuna mixture to a serving bowl with a serving spoon, and surround the bowl with the fried wontons. Serve.

NOTE: To toast the sesame seeds, spread them in a small, dry skillet and toast over medium heat for about 30 seconds or until they darken a shade and smell fragrant.

TUNA SASHIMI BURGERS

When I was in Washington State recently I ate at a beautiful outdoor café on a day when the sun was shining and a gentle breeze wafted off the sparkling ocean. We ordered an intriguing-sounding starter called tuna sliders. They turned out to be small tuna burgers, which I just loved. I developed my own version, which is every bit as good as those I had on the West Coast. **SERVES 6 AS A FIRST COURSE; 3 AS AN ENTRÉE**

12 ounces tuna, cut into ¼-inch dice
    (about 1⅓ cups), see Note

2 tablespoons sesame oil

1 tablespoon minced fresh chives

2 teaspoons soy sauce

1½ teaspoons roasted garlic and red pepper
    spice mixture, see Note

1 teaspoon finely grated peeled fresh ginger

1 teaspoon kosher salt

¼ teaspoon freshly ground white pepper

6 small whole wheat rolls or other small
    soft rolls, halved

2 tablespoons Thai Cream Sauce, page 227

2 tablespoons olive oil

WINE RECOMMENDATION
The sweetness and the oak character of American-style Chardonnay
are a great match for the fish and
ginger components. Try Kendall
Jackson or Cakebread.

BEER RECOMMENDATION
Beers from Japan usually offer
flavors that are more austere and
work well with its spicy cuisine.
I also find there is a slight salty
component to them, which is
pleasing. We recommend Sapporo.

In a mixing bowl, gently but thoroughly combine the tuna, sesame oil, chives, soy sauce, spice mixture, ginger, salt, and pepper.

With dampened palms, form the tuna into 6 thick patties, each approximately 2½ inches in diameter and 1 inch thick.

Spread the roll halves evenly with the Thai cream sauce.

In a medium sauté pan, heat the oil over high heat until very hot but not smoking. Cook the tuna patties for about 1 minute on each side until browned on both sides but still rare in the center. Serve the patties sandwiched in the rolls.

NOTE: If you wrap the tuna in plastic wrap and freeze for about 1 hour, it will be easier to dice. Do not let it freeze completely; the object is to partially freeze it.

Roasted garlic and red pepper spice mix is sold in the Asian section of most supermarkets.

OUR MORTON'S The Steakhouse on Connecticut Avenue in the heart of the District of Columbia is an extremely popular dining spot for politicians and celebrities from the nation's capital. Our guests at this particular Morton's have definite preferences on where they like to be seated. Larry King likes to dine at booth 10, where a painting of him hangs directly overhead. Mr. King's favorite dish is the Morton's Chopped Salad, "chopped fine," along with the swordfish, which used to be on our menu. Senator Orrin Hatch (Republican, Utah) likes table 60 and booth 15, and the restaurant stocks sparkling apple cider just for him. Senator Robert Menendez (Democrat, New Jersey) likes booth 12 and always orders the New York strip cooked medium. The first time founding CEO and Chairman Emeritus of AOL James Kimsey dined at this Morton's, he requested some wasabi with his tuna steak, and a staffer ran out quickly to get some and bring it back. Finally, one of our favorite Morton's regulars, former U.S. solicitor general, the Honorable Theodore B. Olson, "owns" table 14, where he and his wife, Lady Booth Olson, dine every week. ✎

COCKTAIL PARTY MENU

SIRLOIN STEAK TARTARE, PAGE 40

FIRST COURSE LAMB CHOPS, PAGE 37

SMOKED SALMON WEDGES, PAGE 38

TUNA SASHIMI BURGERS, PAGE 43

———

ICED VODKA WITH SIRLOIN GARNISH, PAGE 12

CAIPIRINHA, PAGE 18

OYSTERS ROCKEFELLER

These are a new addition to the Morton's menu, although oysters Rockefeller have been around since the turn of the last century when they were first served at the famed New Orleans eatery Antoine's. Antoine's has never divulged the recipe for its signature dish, but many chefs in and outside of New Orleans have created their own versions, including us. Over the years, our guests asked for the warm oyster appetizer and so we came up with this recipe. It's a big hit with everyone who dines at Morton's and is sure to be an equally successful dish for you. Ask the fishmonger to shuck the oysters for you if you have never done it before; it's a little tricky. If you do this, buy the oysters as close to serving as possible to ensure they are fresh and briny. Refrigerate them as soon as you get home, preferably on a bed of crushed ice.

MAKES 24 OYSTERS

SPINACH SAUCE

2 tablespoons unsalted butter

⅓ cup minced yellow onion

1¾ teaspoons minced garlic

1 teaspoon kosher salt

½ teaspoon freshly ground black pepper

¼ teaspoon freshly grated nutmeg

2 tablespoons all-purpose flour

1¾ cups half-and-half

1 pound frozen spinach, thawed, chopped,
    and squeezed dry

¼ cup Pernod

2 tablespoons finely grated Parmesan cheese

OYSTERS

9 cups rock salt

24 shucked oysters, still in the bottom shells

1½ to 2 cups Hollandaise Sauce, page 47

3 tablespoons finely grated Parmesan cheese

Fresh lemon wedges

WINE RECOMMENDATION

Tokai wines from grapes grown in northern Italy are very round with good fruit and a heavy body that stand up to this pairing and offer great balance. Try one from Livio Felluga.

A low-acid, high-mineral wine, such as Austrian Grüner Veltliner, will bring out the seafood and bacon in this dish without masking the dish's overall aromatics. Jurtschitsch's GrüVe is a good selection.

Preheat the oven to 450°F.

To make the sauce: In a medium saucepan, melt the butter over low heat. Add the onion and garlic and cook for about 5 minutes, stirring, until translucent. Season with the salt, pepper, and nutmeg.

Sprinkle the flour over the mixture and stir to mix. Cook, stirring constantly, for about 4 minutes until incorporated and the aroma is nutty.

recipe continues on next page

Add the half-and-half and cook for 2 to 3 minutes, stirring frequently, until thickened. Raise the heat and bring to a boil. Immediately lower the heat and simmer for about 1 minute.

With the pan off the heat and using an immersion blender or electric mixer, mix for about 1 minute.

Mix in the spinach and Pernod. Stir in the 2 tablespoons grated cheese and cook for 1 to 2 minutes or until the cheese is fully incorporated and hot. You will have about 3 cups.

To cook the oysters: Spread the rock salt in a large baking pan and set the oysters in their shells on top to hold the shells level without wobbling. Spoon 1 generous tablespoon of the spinach mixture evenly over the oysters to cover the oyster meat completely.

Bake for about 15 minutes, or until the spinach sauce bubbles around the edges of the shells and juices are running from the shells.

Remove from the oven. If the baking pan and salt can fit in the broiler, leave the oysters in it. If not, transfer the oysters to a broiler pan.

Turn on the broiler.

Ladle 1 tablespoon of hollandaise sauce and sprinkle some of the 3 tablespoons cheese over each oyster and broil for 30 to 45 seconds, or until the sauce bubbles and the cheese begins to brown lightly.

Transfer the oysters to a serving platter, garnish with lemon wedges, and serve.

HOLLANDAISE SAUCE

Everyone loves rich, tangy hollandaise sauce, and our guests are no exceptions. It's delicious with roast beef as well as with seafood, as in the Oysters Rockefeller on page 45, and with vegetables. Our method for making it is as close to foolproof as you can get: Whisk the eggs constantly over gently simmering water so that they do not scramble, then add the warm, melted butter slowly. Make the sauce shortly before serving; it does not hold well. **MAKES ABOUT 2 CUPS**

5 large egg yolks

1½ cups Clarified Butter, page 227

1½ teaspoons fresh lemon juice

⅛ teaspoon Worcestershire sauce

Dash of Tabasco sauce or other
   hot pepper sauce

¼ teaspoon salt

⅛ teaspoon freshly ground
   white pepper

In the bottom half of a double boiler, bring about 2 inches of water to a boil over high heat. The water should not touch the bottom of the top portion of the double boiler. Reduce the heat to medium so that the water is simmering.

Put the egg yolks and 2 tablespoons of water in the top of the double boiler and set over the simmering water. Whisk the eggs continuously for 2 to 2½ minutes, or until the eggs are thick and foamy and their color lightens. Watch the eggs carefully; they must not scramble and cook. Remove the top of the double boiler from the heat.

In a small saucepan, heat the butter over medium-low heat. Very gradually add half of the warm butter to the eggs, whisking constantly. Add 1 tablespoon of water and continue to whisk as you add the rest of the melted butter and the sauce emulsifies.

Stir in the lemon juice, Worcestershire, Tabasco, salt, and pepper. Return the top of the double boiler to the heat over the simmering water (add more water to the bottom of the double boiler if necessary). Cook gently until the sauce registers 110° to 120°F on an instant-read thermometer. Serve the sauce warm.

STEAMED MUSSELS
WITH GARLIC AND TOMATO

One of the most critical ingredients for this fresh, glorious first course is bread. It's positively essential for sopping up the delicious juices left in the bottom of the dish! You don't want to let even a drop escape. I think of this as summer food, the kind of dish to eat on the deck or patio when no one minds getting a little messy. When I first started preparing mussels years ago, I had to scrub them clean and pull out the wiry "beards" most of them sported. No longer. Today's mussels are very clean, although they still need a good rinse under cool water and you may find an occasional "beard" that needs a good yank. If you feel like turning this appetizer into a soup—and why not?—add cream and curry to the broth until it's the consistency and flavor you like. **SERVES 2**

1½ pounds mussels

1 tablespoon extra-virgin olive oil

2 teaspoons minced shallots

2 teaspoons minced garlic

¾ cup dry white wine

¼ cup bottled clam juice

¼ cup seeded and diced plum tomatoes

Crusty French bread

WINE RECOMMENDATION
Pinot Gris from Alsace has a lot of spicy characteristics that will complement the garlic and pungent seafood flavors. Try one produced by Hugel.

Sherry is also fun. It has higher alcohol than still wine and gives this pairing some "heat," plus it's a natural match with seafood. A good fino sherry is easy to find and works well with this dish. Serve sherry chilled and straight up in three-ounce port-style glasses. Those produced by Tio Pepe and Don Ramón are good choices.

To clean the mussels, scrub them under cool running water. If any have fibers protruding from the shells (called "beards"), pull them out.

In a large deep sauté pan, heat the oil over medium-high heat and when hot, sauté the shallots and garlic for about 2 minutes or until lightly browned. Do not let the garlic burn.

Add the mussels, white wine, clam juice, and tomatoes. Cover and cook over medium heat for about 4 minutes, shaking the pan continuously to toss the mussels as they steam.

Pour the mussels and any pan juices into a large serving bowl. Discard any mussels that do not open. Serve with the bread.

TUNA CANAPÉS

When we host private parties in our boardrooms, we often pass a tray of these tasty, colorful canapés, which disappear in minutes. Be sure to use the best-quality and freshest tuna you can buy. **MAKES 20 CANAPÉS**

9 ounces best-quality tuna, cut into ¼-inch
    dice (about 1 cup)

2 plum tomatoes, cored, seeded, and cut into
    ¼-inch dice (about 1 cup)

1 firm, ripe avocado, cut into ¼-inch dice

1½ tablespoons sesame oil

1½ teaspoons kosher salt

⅛ teaspoon freshly ground white pepper

½ teaspoon fresh lemon juice

1 English cucumber, unpeeled and cut into
    about 20 ¼-inch-thick slices

1 tablespoon store-bought balsamic glaze,
    see Note

1 tablespoon Thai Cream Sauce, page 227

In 3 separate small bowls, put the tuna, tomato, and avocado dice. Add ½ tablespoon of sesame oil to each bowl and season with the salt and the pepper. Add the lemon juice to the avocado. Using a rubber spatula, gently mix the ingredients in each bowl.

Put a cucumber slice on a work surface and scoop ½ teaspoon of tuna on it. Scoop ½ teaspoon of avocado and another of tomato next to the tuna so that all three are lined up next to each other. If this is too fussy, layer the tuna, avocado and tomato on the cucumber slices. At the restaurant, we line up the ½ teaspoonfuls of ingredients next to each other in a tablespoon and invert this onto a cucumber slice.

Repeat to make approximately 20 canapés and arrange them on a platter. Do not prepare more than 1 hour before serving.

Before serving, drizzle the canapés with the balsamic glaze and the Thai cream sauce.

NOTE: Roland Balsamic Glaze is available in supermarkets. It's a concentrated sauce made with balsamic vinegar that we use in the restaurant. You may choose another brand or use your favorite balsamic vinegar (aged is best) or balsamic-based vinaigrette, instead.

KEY LIME MARINATED SEAFOOD

I buy fish and seafood from L. Isaacson and Stein Fish Market at 800 West Fulton Market Street in Chicago. The market sells mainly to the restaurant trade but welcomes anyone who wants good, fresh fish. Count me among them! One of the experts there told me that in Mexico kingfish is a popular choice for marinated seafood (also known as ceviche) because it's pleasingly firm and is not too hard on the pocketbook. A kind of mackerel, kingfish looks a little gray when raw, but after marinating it turns a pleasing white. The acid in the lime juice actually "cooks" it so no one is eating raw fish. Key limes make a big difference here so try to use them. They have a little more punch than other limes. Ceviche is so high in acid that wine is usually not a good match, but an acidic cocktail is great. **SERVES 6 TO 8**

1 cup fresh Key lime juice (8 or 9 limes), see Note

½ cup finely chopped red bell pepper

2 tablespoons finely chopped jalapeño pepper

½ cup finely chopped red onion

1 teaspoon salt

1 teaspoon freshly ground black pepper

1½ pounds fresh kingfish or other firm, white fish fillet, cut into ¼-inch cubes or slivers

6 ounces large shrimp (21–25 count), peeled, deveined, and each sliced diagonally into 5 pieces

1 tablespoon chopped fresh cilantro

COCKTAIL RECOMMENDATION
Key Lime Margarita, page 17

BEER RECOMMENDATION
Lager will offer a crisp mouthfeel and refreshing finish for this spicy dish. We suggest Corona or Lone Star.

In a glass or ceramic bowl, stir together the lime juice, bell pepper, jalapeño pepper, onion, salt, and pepper. Add the fish and the shrimp and mix gently to coat with the marinade. Cover and refrigerate for at least 4 hours but no longer than 6 hours.

Just before serving, remove the bowl from the refrigerator and gently stir in the cilantro. Serve in small bowls.

NOTE: Bottled Key lime juice does not work well in this recipe in terms of flavor and acidity. Use only fresh Key lime juice (or fresh lime juice from ordinary limes if Key limes are not in season).

WARM BLUE-CHEESE DIP

Donna Rundle, our manager of restaurant services, donated this recipe for the book. It plays on two of the flavors we love at Morton's: blue cheese and smoked bacon. Once you try it, you'll be addicted. Everyone we know is mad for it, and it's as amazing with raw vegetables or crackers as with good French bread. Donna says she got the idea for the dip when, on the way to a family reunion in Kansas, she passed through Newton, Iowa, where Maytag blue cheese is produced. She bought a big wheel of cheese and then set about coming up with any number of ways to serve it. This was one of her favorites. **SERVES 8 TO 10**

8 slices hickory-smoked bacon, diced

2 cloves garlic, minced

8 ounces cream cheese, softened

¼ cup heavy cream

4 ounces crumbled blue cheese

2 tablespoons chopped fresh chives

2 tablespoons chopped almonds

Crackers, sliced baguette, or trimmed fresh vegetables, for serving

WINE RECOMMENDATION
Cabernets from Chile tend to have a great vegetal character and strong tannins. They can be drunk young and taste great with this dip. Concha y Toro and Casa Lapostolle Apalta Vineyard are reliable producers.

COCKTAIL RECOMMENDATION
Port Sangria, page 24

Preheat the oven to 350°F.

In a nonstick skillet, cook the bacon over medium-high heat for about 8 minutes or until nearly crisp. Drain the bacon and wipe the skillet dry.

Return the bacon to the pan, add the garlic, and cook over medium heat for about 3 minutes longer or until the bacon is crisp. Take care the garlic does not burn. Drain on paper towels.

In the bowl of an electric mixer fitted with the paddle attachment, beat the cream cheese until smooth. Add the cream and beat well to mix. Fold in the bacon, garlic, blue cheese, and chives.

Transfer to a 2-cup baking dish, top evenly with the almonds, and bake for about 30 minutes or until heated through.

Serve with crackers, baguette slices, or vegetables.

MORTON'S CENTER-CUT ICEBERG SALAD

This is one of those salads that proves the old adage that there is "nothing new under the sun"... nor in the restaurant business. Cold, crisp iceberg lettuce wedge salads with blue cheese dressing enjoyed a heyday in the 1940s, '50s, and '60s and then the salad disappeared, to be found only in a very few outposts of old-time traditions. But it's back with a vengeance and our guests are thrilled. It's a robust, refreshing salad, with enough bold flavors to earn a spot on our menu—and in our hearts. You will note that we cut the wedges from the center of the heads for the crunchiest part of the lettuce. **SERVES 2**

1 head of iceberg lettuce, about 1½ pounds

⅓ cup Blue Cheese Dressing, opposite

2 to 3 slices crisp-cooked bacon, crumbled
   (about 3 tablespoons)

1 hard-cooked large egg, chopped
   (about 3 tablespoons)

3 tablespoons chopped tomato

3 tablespoons crumbled blue cheese

Remove any wilted outside leaves from the lettuce. Strike the bottom of the lettuce head on a flat surface to loosen the core and then pull out the core.

Slice four 2-inch-thick wedges from the center section of the head. Discard or reserve the rest for another use. Put 2 wedges on each of 2 serving plates.

Ladle the dressing across the wedges so that it runs over one side. Sprinkle with the bacon, egg, tomato, and blue cheese and serve immediately.

BLUE-CHEESE DRESSING

This dressing would be equally delicious with just about any other green salad, with sliced tomatoes, or served as a dip. We serve it with the iceberg lettuce salad in keeping with the tradition of that old-time dish. You won't need all you make here, but as is true of certain recipes, it's easier to make more than you need than to work with small amounts of ingredients. **MAKES ABOUT 1½ CUPS**

1 cup mayonnaise, see Note

10 tablespoons sour cream

2 tablespoons buttermilk

½ teaspoon Durkee Famous Sauce, see Note

¼ teaspoon seasoned salt

Salt and freshly ground black pepper

3½ ounces crumbled blue cheese (about ¾ cup)

In a mixing bowl, whisk together the mayonnaise and sour cream. Add the buttermilk, Durkee sauce, and seasoned salt. Whisk until well mixed. Season to taste with salt and pepper and whisk again.

Using a rubber spatula, gently fold in the blue cheese. Transfer to a storage container with a tight-fitting lid and refrigerate for up to 4 days.

NOTE: Use real mayonnaise, such as Kraft or Best Foods, and not a related product such as Miracle Whip or light mayonnaise. At Morton's we use Kraft Real Mayonnaise. When writing this book, we tried making the dressing with Miracle Whip, and the finished product turned thin and milky when it was stored for more than a day.

Durkee Famous Sauce is sold in many supermarkets. It's a vinegar-flavored, mustard-mayonnaise type of sauce.

TOMATO, MOZZARELLA, AND PROSCIUTTO SALAD

This classic salad is at its very best in the summertime, when the tomatoes are ripe and juicy and everyone's garden overflows with basil. If you can find handmade mozzarella, it makes all the difference here. Luckily, it's not too hard to find nowadays; it's available at many supermarkets packed in water. Fran Drescher is expecially fond of this salad. She is known for her long-running role on the television series The Nanny, *but she is also a* New York Times *bestselling author, a cancer survivor, and in 2008 was appointed Public Diplomatic Envoy by the U.S. State Department.*

SERVES 2

4 romaine lettuce leaves

2 large beefsteak tomatoes, cored and each
    cut into 4 slices

8 ounces fresh mozzarella cheese, cut into
    8 slices

8 to 10 paper-thin slices high-quality
    prosciutto (about 1 ounce)

8 large fresh basil leaves

Olive oil

Balsamic vinegar

Salt and freshly ground black pepper

Line each of 2 salad plates with lettuce leaves. Shingle the tomato slices over the lettuce and top with mozzarella slices and prosciutto, shingled also so that they overlap. Tuck the basil leaves between the cheese and ham.

Drizzle the olive oil and vinegar over the salad and sprinkle with salt and pepper to taste. If you prefer, you can serve the oil and vinegar on the side and let your guests dress their own salad.

MIXED GREEN SALAD
WITH GRILLED SHRIMP

When executive chef Chris Rook put this salad together for a wine dinner series, guests went crazy. You'll understand why when you try it, as the ingredients seem made for each other. The sweet grilled shrimp is a perfect foil for the apples, nuts, and cheese. **SERVES 4**

4 jumbo shrimp (6–8 count), peeled
   and deveined, tails intact
Seasoning salt
Olive oil
1 Granny Smith apple

8 ounces mixed field greens (about 8 cups)
½ cup crumbled blue cheese (about 2 ounces)
¼ cup toasted chopped walnuts
½ cup Dijon Vinaigrette, page 224

Preheat the broiler.

Put the shrimp on a broiler pan, sprinkle with seasoning salt, and brush lightly with olive oil. Broil for about 2 minutes on each side or until they begin to turn pink and are almost cooked through.

Remove the shrimp from the broiler and heat the oven to 500°F. Let the shrimp cool. Meanwhile, peel and core the apple and cut it into ¼-inch-thick slices.

Butterfly each shrimp by splitting them down the middle starting at the tail and cutting along the inside curve. Do not cut all the way through.

Return the shrimp to the broiler pan or another baking dish and heat in the hot oven for about 2 minutes or until pink and cooked through.

In a large mixing bowl, toss the greens with the apples, cheese, and walnuts. Drizzle with the vinaigrette and toss until well mixed. Divide the salad among 4 salad plates and top each salad with a shrimp.

MAINE LOBSTER AND AVOCADO SALAD

When you put two elegant ingredients such as lobster and avocado together, you are in for a sumptuous treat. Few salads could be easier but the end result is refreshing and nothing if not refined. This could be a first course or a light lunch. **SERVES 2**

¼ cup minced celery

3 tablespoons mayonnaise

1½ tablespoons ketchup

½ teaspoon fresh lime juice

¼ teaspoon freshly ground black pepper

⅛ teaspoon salt

1½ ounces cremini mushrooms,
  very thinly sliced

10 ounces fresh or frozen cooked lobster meat,
  cut into 1-inch-thick pieces

4 large red-leaf lettuce leaves

4 Boston lettuce leaves

6 Belgian endive leaves

1 firm, ripe avocado

1 plum tomato, halved and then cut into
  6 wedges

In a small bowl, mix together the celery, mayonnaise, ketchup, lime juice, pepper, and salt. Gently fold in the mushrooms and lobster.

In shallow soup bowls, lay 2 red-leaf lettuce and 2 Boston lettuce leaves in the bottom of each bowl. Arrange 3 endive leaves in each bowl, pointing outward toward the rim.

Halve the avocado and remove the pit. Mound half of the salad in each avocado half and place one in each bowl. Garnish with the tomato wedges.

MORTON'S ASIAN SLAW

Executive chef Chris Rock put this together one day, using packaged slaw mix and a package of ramen noodles. He browns almonds and the rice noodles in butter and tosses them with a sweet-and-sour dressing. This slaw is tasty!

SERVES 6 TO 8

One 3-ounce package Maruchan Oriental Flavor Ramen Noodles and seasoning packet

3 tablespoons unsalted butter

2 tablespoons slivered almonds

24 ounces bagged broccoli slaw mix or your favorite slaw mix

¼ cup roasted sunflower seeds, see Note

½ cup apple cider vinegar

¼ cup packed light brown sugar

¾ cup sunflower or canola oil

Break the dried noodles into small pieces.

In a small sauté pan, melt the butter over medium-low heat and when melted, add the broken noodles and almonds and sauté for 5 to 7 minutes or until golden brown. Transfer to a paper-towel-lined plate and cover with paper towels to absorb any excess butter.

In a mixing bowl, toss the slaw mix with the sunflower seeds.

In another bowl, stir together the vinegar, brown sugar, and the contents of the seasoning packet until the sugar dissolves. Add the oil and whisk well.

Pour the dressing over the slaw and mix well. Stir in the noodles and almonds. Serve right away or refrigerate for up to 24 hours. This is best made at least 2 or 3 hours ahead of time.

NOTE: To toast the sunflower seeds, which accentuates their flavor, spread them in a dry skillet over medium-high heat for about 30 seconds or until they darken a shade and are fragrant. You can also buy toasted sunflower seeds.

✎ CELEBRITY CLIP ✎

TWELVE DAYS after turning thirty-two years old, Stacy Ferguson, better known to the music world as Fergie, celebrated her birthday with a family-filled party in the private-dining boardroom at Morton's The Steakhouse in Santa Ana, California. The well-known lead singer of the Black Eyed Peas and solo artist was joined by fiancé Josh Duhamel, who helped Fergie greet her guests at the front door: sister Dana, her mother, father, stepfather, and grandmother. On the menu that night were crab legs, oysters on the half shell, broiled scallops wrapped in bacon with apricot chutney, and chocolate soufflé . . . as well as a birthday serenade. ✎

MID-WINTER SUNDAY SUPPER
MENU FOR A CROWD

KLAUS'S SIRLOIN CHILI, PAGE 80

MORTON'S CENTER-CUT ICEBERG SALAD, PAGE 54

FRENCH BREAD OR HOT CORNBREAD

MRS. ARTINIAN'S CARROT CAKE, PAGE 209

EDIE'S CHOPPED VEGETABLE SALAD

Morton's president, Edie Ames, contributed this lovely salad to the book. It's a pretty, light vegetable salad perfect for a party or to have on hand for the family. Use the freshest veggies available; but you don't have to follow our list to a "T." Think of it as inspiration. **SERVES 10**

½ cup finely chopped radishes (4 to 5 radishes)

½ cup finely chopped carrot (1 small carrot)

½ cup finely chopped celery (1 small rib celery)

½ cup finely chopped peeled zucchini (one 4- to 5-inch zucchini)

½ cup finely chopped peeled yellow squash (one 4- to 5-inch squash)

½ cup finely chopped peeled English cucumber (about 5 inches of cucumber)

½ cup shelled edamame beans (about 2 ½ ounces)

½ cup finely chopped red bell pepper ½ small pepper)

One 14-ounce can hearts of palm, drained, cut into ¼-inch-thick slices

One 14-ounce can artichoke hearts, packed in water, drained, quartered

About 1 cup Dijon Vinaigrette, page 224

1 head of iceberg lettuce, coarsely chopped (about 8 cups)

½ cup seeded and finely chopped tomatoes

Salt and freshly ground black pepper

In a large mixing bowl, toss together the radishes, carrot, celery, zucchini, yellow squash, cucumber, edamame beans, bell pepper, hearts of palm, and artichoke hearts. Pour the dressing over the vegetables and mix well. Cover and refrigerate for 4 to 6 hours.

In a large salad bowl, toss together the lettuce, tomatoes, marinated vegetables, and any marinade in the bowl. Add more dressing, if needed. Season to taste with salt and pepper.

WARM STEAK SALAD
WITH ASIAN DRESSING

A warm steak salad is a perfect solution for lunch when you want to serve something a little special but don't have time for a lot of fuss. The vegetables taste wonderful with the Asian-inspired dressing **SERVES 4**

DRESSING

2 tablespoons plus 2 teaspoons soy sauce

2 tablespoons peanut oil

2 tablespoons sesame oil

2 tablespoons white rice wine vinegar

½ teaspoon finely minced fresh ginger

½ teaspoon finely minced garlic

½ teaspoon crushed red pepper flakes

SALAD

1 pound bok choy

8 cups torn romaine lettuce

6 cups chopped iceberg lettuce

1 medium carrot, peeled and cut into very thin strips

1 medium red bell pepper, seeded, membranes removed and cut into very thin strips

5 to 6 scallions, white and green parts, chopped

½ cup Clarified Butter, page 227

2 pounds tenderloin tips or tails, sliced into strips about ½ inch thick

4 teaspoons toasted sesame seeds

WINE RECOMMENDATION

When you serve red meat with vinegar, pairing it with wine is a challenge—but certainly not impossible. The choice here is to go with a dessert wine. The density of the late-harvest wine with its earthiness will complement the steak, and its high level of brix will calm down the dressing. I recommend a late-harvest semillion from Mer Soliel called Late. Serve it well chilled.

To make the dressing: whisk together the soy sauce, peanut oil, sesame oil, and vinegar. Add the ginger, garlic, and red pepper flakes and stir well. Set aside for at least 1 hour and up to 24 hours if possible for the best flavor. Put bok choy into an ice bath until crisp for about 30 minutes.

To prepare the salad: Cut the green ends of the bok choy into pieces about 1½ inches wide. Continue cutting the stalks on the bias into ½-inch-thick slices. Transfer to a bowl filled with ice water and let it crisp for about 30 minutes. Spin dry. In a large mixing bowl, toss together the bok choy, romaine, iceberg lettuce, carrot, bell pepper, and scallions.

In a large skillet, heat the butter over medium-high heat. Cook the tenderloin tips in the hot butter for about 90 seconds, turning once, or until medium-rare. Transfer the steak to a shallow bowl and add about ¼ cup of the dressing. Toss to coat the meat.

Drizzle about ¼ cup of the dressing over the salad greens and toss to mix. Pile the salad on 4 serving plates and top each with strips of steak. Garnish with sesame seeds.

NEW YORK STRIP STEAK AND BEEFSTEAK TOMATO SALAD

This towering salad straddles the line between a salad and a sandwich, albeit a breadless one! We love it for its marriage of glorious summer flavors as well as for its impressive presentation—which looks far more complicated than it is. **SERVES 4**

DRESSING

¼ cup red wine vinegar

1½ teaspoons sugar

2 teaspoons crushed dried oregano

¾ cup vegetable oil

SALAD

Twelve 4-ounce pieces New York strip steak ends

Seasoned salt

4 tomatoes

4 leaves romaine lettuce

Twelve ⅛-inch-thick slices red onion

8 ounces crumbled blue cheese

WINE RECOMMENDATION

The steak, tomato, and cheese in this dish transport you directly to Florence, Italy, and the wine should be from that part of the world. Sangiovese will stand up to the beef and soothe the acid in the tomatoes, while offering earth tones and tannins to balance the cheese. My paring would be Ruffino Gold Label, and Chianti Classico Riserva.

To make the dressing: In a mixing bowl, whisk together the vinegar, sugar, and oregano until the sugar dissolves. Slowly add the oil, whisking constantly, until fully incorporated. Set aside. Store in a lidded container at room temperature for up to 5 days.

To make the salad: Preheat the broiler.

Season the steak on both sides with seasoned salt. Lay the steak in a broiling pan and broil for 1 to 1½ minutes, turning once, or until medium rare. Set aside, covered, to keep warm.

Core the tomatoes and then cut into ¾-inch-thick slices.

Lay a lettuce leaf on each of 4 serving plates. Arrange alternating slices of tomato, onion, and beef on top of the lettuce. Drizzle each salad with about 1½ tablespoons of dressing and top with blue cheese. Serve immediately.

SUMMERTIME GAZPACHO

SOUPS AND SANDWICHES

MORTON'S FIVE-ONION SOUP

—

SUMMERTIME GAZPACHO

—

BOSTON SWEET CORN AND
LOBSTER CHOWDER

—

MINNESOTA WILD RICE AND
MUSHROOM SOUP

—

KLAUS'S SIRLOIN CHILI

CHICKEN SALAD SANDWICHES

—

PRIME RIB FRENCH DIP SANDWICHES

—

Matt Birk's Favorite
MORTON'S TWO-FISTED BACON
CHEESEBURGER

—

SMOKED SALMON CLUB

—

Willie Randolph's Favorite
CRABCAKE "BLT"
WITH DILL-CAPER SAUCE

MORTON'S FIVE-ONION SOUP

Morton's regulars have been able to find this onion soup on our lunch menu for years but it's only recently that we added it to the dinner menu. I am not sure what took us so long, but our dinner guests are pleased as punch. Steaming, hot bowls blanketed with melting cheese fly out of the kitchen! The Madeira coupled with the five different kinds of onions (among which we count garlic) give this soup a hint of sweetness that is almost impossible to resist. But why would anyone want to? **SERVES 10**

1 tablespoon olive oil

1¼ pounds Spanish onions (about 2 large), thinly sliced

1 large red onion, thinly sliced

1 small leek, halved, thinly sliced, and well rinsed

3 to 4 shallots, thinly sliced

½ cup minced garlic (about 20 cloves)

5 tablespoons dry sherry

¼ cup Madeira wine

1½ teaspoons beef base, see Note page 81

1½ teaspoons chicken base, see Note page 81

1 teaspoon fresh thyme leaves

¾ teaspoon herbes de Provence

1 small bay leaf

1¾ quarts (7 cups) reconstituted store-bought demi-glace, see Note, page 117, or beef broth

1 teaspoon salt

½ teaspoon freshly ground white pepper

Croutons for Five-Onion Soup, page 74

1¼ pounds Swiss or Jarlsberg cheese, grated or shredded

Chopped fresh flat-leaf parsley, for serving

In a deep stockpot, heat the olive oil over medium-low heat. Add both types of onions, the leek, shallots, and garlic and cook very slowly, loosely covered, for 30 to 35 minutes or until the onions release their juices, are very soft and syrupy, and are lightly browned.

Add the sherry, Madeira, beef and chicken base, thyme, herbes de Provence, and bay leaf. Raise the heat to medium and bring to a simmer. Simmer for 4 to 5 minutes to cook off the alcohol.

Stir in the demi-glace and bring to a boil. Lower the heat and simmer, partially covered, for about 20 minutes.

Preheat the broiler.

Remove the bay leaf, adjust the seasoning with salt and pepper, and ladle the soup into

recipe continues on page 74

10 broiler-safe onion soup crocks. Lay 2 croutons on top of each bowl of soup and sprinkle the cheese over the croutons. The cheese should cover both the croutons and the soup.

Working in batches, broil the soup crocks 2 to 3 inches from the heat source for about 2 minutes, or until the cheese browns and the soup bubbles around the sides. Use heavy oven mitts to handle the crocks and take great care removing the crocks from the broiler. Garnish each bowl with parsley and serve the soup immediately.

CROUTONS FOR FIVE-ONION SOUP

MAKES 20 TO 25 CROUTONS

One 18- to 20-inch-long baguette or
4 Portuguese or Milano rolls

Preheat the oven to 450°F.

Cut the bread on the diagonal into croutons that measure about 2½ inches long, 1½ inches wide, and ½ inch thick. Spread the croutons on a baking sheet and bake for 4 to 6 minutes or until golden brown. Turn and bake for 4 to 6 minutes on the other side, or until golden brown.

Remove from the oven, slide the croutons onto a cool pan or rack and let cool. Use right away or store in a lidded container for up to 3 days.

SUMMERTIME GRILL MENU

SUMMERTIME GAZPACHO, PAGE 75

MORTON'S TWO-FISTED BACON CHEESEBURGER, PAGE 86

MORTON'S ASIAN SLAW, PAGE 62

BLUE-CHEESE FRENCH FRIES, PAGE 198

DOUBLE CHOCOLATE MOUSSE, PAGE 204

———

PORT SANGRIA, PAGE 24

SUMMERTIME GAZPACHO

When vegetables are at their best in the summer, try this classic soup. It's cool and refreshing—just what you want when the mercury climbs. As others have said, it truly is like "salad in a soup bowl." We like to make it with Sacramento tomato juice, but for a little more kick try Bloody Mary mix. **SERVES 4**

1¼ cups chicken broth

1¼ cups tomato juice

1 cup finely chopped peeled and seeded cucumber

Generous ½ cup finely chopped yellow onion

Generous ½ cup finely chopped green bell pepper

2 tablespoons plus 1 teaspoon white wine vinegar

Salt and freshly ground black pepper

2 dashes of Tabasco or other hot pepper sauce, or more to taste

2 dashes of Worcestershire sauce

2 tablespoons chopped fresh cilantro

WINE RECOMMENDATION

French Sauvignon Blanc is not so much citrusy but instead its main components are earthy, grassy, and mineral-like, elements that mirror those in the gazpacho. The low acid balances the high acid of the tomatoes. Look for a Sancerre.

Reisling can temper the acid, too, and offer a refreshing match that provides both spice and fruit. German-style Rieslings are generally lower in alcohol, and so they don't mask the delicate flavors of the food. Try Dr. Loosen Riesling (Kabinett) from Germany.

In a large bowl, stir together the chicken broth, tomato juice, cucumber, onion, bell pepper, and vinegar. Season to taste with salt and pepper. Add the hot pepper sauce and Worcestershire sauce, taste, and adjust the seasonings.

Cover the bowl and refrigerate for at least 3 hours and up to 24 hours. Serve cold in chilled bowls, garnished with the cilantro.

BOSTON SWEET CORN
AND LOBSTER CHOWDER

We named this for the grand old city of Boston because we immediately think of New England when we think of chowder. New England summer sweet corn is as good as it gets, and while you can make this with frozen corn kernels, make it with fresh corn for an extra-special treat. The lobster, pulled from the deep cold waters off New England's coast, makes this a pleasing and very indulgent soup. It could be a first course or a light meal. **SERVES 6**

2 small live lobsters (1 ¼ to 1 ½ pounds each; sometimes called chick lobsters)

3 tablespoons salted butter

¼ cup all-purpose flour

2 slices bacon, cut into ¼-inch dice

¾ cup chopped celery

½ cup chopped yellow onion

1½ packed cups corn kernels, fresh (about 3 ears) or frozen

1 bay leaf

⅛ teaspoon dried thyme or 1 teaspoon chopped fresh thyme

3 cups heavy cream

1 pound red-skinned all-purpose potatoes, cut into eighths

½ teaspoon salt

¼ teaspoon freshly ground black pepper

Dry sherry, optional

Chopped fresh chives, for serving

In a large, deep pot, bring 3 quarts water to a boil. Plunge the lobsters, head first, into the boiling water, cover the pot, and poach for about 10 minutes or until the lobster are bright red and cooked.

Using tongs, remove the lobsters and put in a bowl to cool. Reserve the poaching liquid.

When cool enough to handle, pull the lobster meat from the claws and tail of the lobsters. Divide the meat into 6 equal portions and set aside.

Cut the shells into small pieces and then return them to the pot with the poaching liquid. Bring to a boil over high heat, reduce the heat slightly, and simmer rapidly for about 20 minutes, partially covered, until slightly reduced. Strain the poaching liquid through a sieve and discard the shells.

recipe continues on next page

In a small sauté pan, melt the butter over medium heat. Sprinkle the flour over the butter, stirring constantly for 2 to 3 minutes until the mixture is smooth and turns golden brown. Set the roux aside to cool.

In a large stockpot, sauté the bacon over medium heat for 2 to 3 minutes, or until the fat renders and begins to brown slightly. Add the celery and onion, partially cover, and cook for about 5 minutes longer or until the vegetables are soft and tender but not browned.

Add the corn, bay leaf, thyme, and 5 cups of the poaching liquid. (Reserve 1 cup of the remaining liquid separately.) Bring the liquid to a boil over high heat, reduce the heat slightly, and simmer rapidly, uncovered, for about 20 minutes or until reduced by half.

Add the roux to the pot and whisk until smooth and blended. Stir in the cream until blended.

Add the potatoes and bring to a simmer. Reduce the heat to low and cook for about 15 minutes, partially covered, or until tender. Add the salt and pepper and a few drops of sherry, if desired. Discard the bay leaf.

In a saucepan, heat the reserved 1 cup poaching liquid over medium-high heat. When simmering, use a small strainer or slotted spoon to dunk each portion of lobster meat into it to heat through. Drain and transfer to one of 6 warmed soup bowls. Ladle a generous cup of soup over the lobster. Garnish with the chives.

NOTE: Any leftover poaching liquid can be frozen and used as a base for any seafood soup or sauce.

If you slice the potatoes ahead of time, keep them submerged in a bowl of cold water until ready to use. This will keep them fresh and white.

MINNESOTA WILD RICE AND MUSHROOM SOUP

Wild rice is not actually rice but seeds of marsh grasses, and as such it takes longer to cook than you might expect. Follow the package instructions for cooking it. (You can do this a day in advance.) It grows most plentifully in the many lakes of our northern-tier Midwestern states, although it's now farmed in Canada and California, too. With a little patience, you will end up with a glorious fall soup bursting with earthy flavors. **SERVES 8 TO 10**

½ cup wild rice

3 tablespoons unsalted butter

1 cup chopped celery

¾ cup chopped yellow onion

2 cloves garlic, minced

1 pound medium white mushrooms,
    sliced ¼ inch thick

8 ounces cremini mushrooms,
    sliced ¼ inch thick

8 ounces shiitake mushrooms, stemmed and
    sliced ¼-inch thick

5 tablespoons all-purpose flour

1 quart (4 cups) heavy cream

¼ teaspoon freshly ground black pepper

WINE RECOMMENDATION
Chablis is more straightforward and crisp than American Chardonnay and won't get in the way. Its great mineral and earth components work with this soup. Try Olivier Leflaive from France.

BEER RECOMMENDATION
Leinenkugel's is an excellent beer producer from Wisconsin. The honey and hoppy flavors are a welcome pairing with the mushrooms and denseness of the dish. We like Leinenkugel's Honey Weiss.

Cook the wild rice according to the package instructions. Strain the rice and reserve the liquid. Add more water if needed to measure 2 cups of cooking liquid. You will have about 2 cups of cooked rice.

In a large stockpot, melt the butter over medium heat. Add the celery, onion, and garlic and sauté for 8 to 10 minutes, or until the vegetables soften but are not browned.

Raise the heat to medium-high. Add the mushrooms and stir continuously for 10 to 12 minutes, or until they release their liquid and soften. Sprinkle the flour over the mushrooms and stir to blend to make sure there are no lumps. Cook for about 1 minute.

Add the cream and mix gently but thoroughly. Add the cooked rice and the 2 cups reserved liquid. Simmer gently for about 5 minutes to heat thoroughly and thicken. Season to taste with pepper and serve, ladled into soup bowls.

KLAUS'S SIRLOIN CHILI

This is one of my most requested recipes and I make it often in the wintertime: on New Year's Day, on Super Bowl Sunday, or for just about any cold-weather get-together. The secret is to chop the meat yourself (or ask the butcher to do it for you) rather than use pre-ground beef. The texture and beefy flavor is much better. You actually chew chunks of meat when you eat this chili. Don't rush this dish but let it simmer slowly so all its goodness has plenty of time to develop. I like to serve the chili with sour cream, chopped onions, shredded cheese, and jalapeño peppers. This takes a lot of garlic: six tablespoons. For this, you will need approximately eighteen cloves of garlic, which is about two whole heads. You can buy garlic already peeled in some markets. Don't buy it already chopped; pre-chopped garlic tends to taste bitter. **SERVES 10 TO 12**

¼ cup vegetable oil

2 pounds yellow onions, chopped (about 4 cups)

6 tablespoons minced garlic (about 18 cloves)

3 pounds boneless chuck roast, trimmed of fat and silver skin, cut into ¼-inch dice

¼ cup chili powder

2 tablespoons ground cumin

2 teaspoons freshly ground black pepper

Four 14½-ounce cans diced tomatoes with juice

Four 16-ounce cans spicy chili beans, such as Allen's

2 cups water

Two 8-ounce cans tomato sauce

2 tablespoons beef base, see Note

2 bay leaves

Salt

WINE RECOMMENDATION
For all the strong flavors in Klaus's bold chili, you need a big wine without too much alcohol. It should taste of some ripe stone fruits to bring out elements other than the beef. Washington State Syrah is a great choice. We suggest Chateau Ste. Michelle and Leonetti.

BEER RECOMMENDATION
A good Belgian, Czech, or German pilsner has a good, clean yeasty finish, ideal with this dish—and refreshing, to boot. Our choice is the Czech brew Pilsner Urquell.

In a large stockpot, heat the oil over medium-low heat. Add the onions and garlic and cook for about 8 minutes, stirring occasionally, until the onions start to soften.

Add the beef, raise the heat to medium-high, and stir for about 5 minutes as it begins to lose its pink color. Add the chili powder, cumin, and pepper and cook for 1 to 2 minutes to let the flavors develop.

Add the tomatoes and their juice, beans and their juice, water, tomato sauce, and beef base. Stir to mix well and then add the bay leaves. Stir gently.

Reduce the heat to low and let the chili simmer gently for about 2 hours, or until the meat is tender. Stir frequently so that the chili does not stick to the bottom of the pot. Adjust the heat up or down to maintain a slow simmer.

Thin the chili with water, if necessary, and add salt to taste. It might not be necessary, as the beans are salty. Remove the bay leaves and serve.

The chili can be cooled and refrigerated for up to 3 days and frozen for up to 1 month. Reheat it gently, stirring frequently.

NOTE: Beef and chicken bases are available in local supermarkets, or you can search for them online. We use bases from Bear Creek Country Kitchens. Another good brand is Superior Touch Better Than Bouillon. The pastelike products are sold in small jars and are intensely flavored. Measure carefully, and taste for salt, as they tend to be salty.

Easy Lunch Menu

Tomato, Mozzarella, and Prosciutto Salad, page 57

Boston Sweet Corn and Lobster Chowder, page 77

Hot biscuits

Honey-Glazed Apple Pastry, page 214

———

Heavenly Pear Mortini, page 16

CHICKEN SALAD SANDWICHES

Just about everyone makes chicken salad, and what makes this one stand out is that we begin with a whole chicken, which we poach gently in a flavored stock. The chicken is mixed with tart-sweet Granny Smith apples and dried cranberries. As delicious as the chicken salad is, the bread truly makes the sandwich. We recommend you slice it from a good Tuscan loaf, a rustic round farmstead loaf, or a great pumpernickel. **SERVES 4**

CHICKEN

One 3- to 3½-pound chicken

1 cup coarsely chopped carrot

1 cup coarsely chopped celery

1 cup coarsely chopped onion

2 whole cloves garlic

1 bay leaf

1 teaspoon salt

¼ teaspoon freshly ground black pepper

CHICKEN SALAD

½ cup peeled and finely chopped Granny
　　Smith or similar green apple

½ cup finely chopped celery

2 tablespoons dried cranberries

¼ cup mayonnaise

1 tablespoon fresh lemon juice

¼ teaspoon Worcestershire sauce

¼ teaspoon salt

⅛ teaspoon freshly ground black pepper

SANDWICH

8 slices hearty country-style bread

8 lettuce leaves

2 plum tomatoes, cored and thinly sliced

2 avocados, pitted and sliced

Chopped fresh flat-leaf parsley, for serving

To cook the chicken: In a large stockpot, cover the chicken with about 10 cups water. Add the carrot, celery, onion, garlic, bay leaf, salt, and pepper. Bring to a boil over medium-high heat, reduce the heat, and simmer for 50 to 60 minutes or until the chicken is cooked through. Adjust the heat up or down to maintain the simmer.

Remove the stockpot from the heat and once the chicken cools slightly, remove it from the cooking liquid. Set the chicken aside for about 30 minutes (no longer), or until cool enough to handle. Strain the cooking liquid, discard the solids, and use the liquid as you would chicken broth.

To make the chicken salad: Remove the skin, bones, and gristle from the chicken. Cut the meat into small cubes, about ½ inch square. You will have about 4 cups.

In a mixing bowl, toss together the apple, celery, and cranberries. Stir in the mayonnaise, lemon juice, and Worcestershire sauce. Gently fold in the chicken. Season with salt and pepper. Use right away or cover and refrigerate for up to 1 day. (We think it tastes best if allowed to mellow in the refrigerator for 8 to 24 hours.)

To make the sandwiches: Toast the bread and line 4 slices with 2 lettuce leaves and 2 tomato slices each. Spoon the chicken salad on top of the tomatoes and top with avocado slices and chopped parsley. Sandwich with the other slices of bread and cut each sandwich on the diagonal.

✎ CELEBRITY CLIP ✎

PRESIDENT GEORGE H. W. BUSH is a very special and regular guest at Morton's. The former president has dined with us in many cities, including Washington, D.C.; Scottsdale, Arizona (where he was interviewed on local television and talked about his favorite Morton's entrées); New York City; and his hometown of Houston, Texas. When we opened a second Morton's in downtown Houston, the former president and first lady joined us for the kickoff party that benefited the *Houston Read Commission,* in honor of Mrs. Bush's extensive work worldwide improving literacy. We toiled feverishly for weeks with the Secret Service to make certain the president could enter the restaurant undetected by the public and with no fanfare, but President Bush turned the tables on us. After greeting the invited dignitaries and others in the private-dining boardroom, he walked into the main dining room and welcomed nearly all of the 350 guests attending the event. We should not have been surprised. Over the years, he has often approached tables of guests to say hello, and if there is a special request for an introduction, he graciously complies. It's no wonder that he is one of our truly favorite Morton's guests. ✎

PRIME RIB FRENCH DIP SANDWICHES

We serve these robust sandwiches at lunch, although some guests ask for them at supper time—and what a great way to use leftover or deli roast beef. When you serve the small cups of au jus with the sandwiches, urge everyone to dig in! The au jus cools quickly. **SERVES 4**

Four 6-inch lengths of baguette

2 cups Au Jus, page 229, plus more for serving

2 pounds cooked boneless prime rib, sliced

12 slices Provolone cheese (about 12 ounces)

4 sprigs fresh watercress

WINE RECOMMENDATION

This sandwich screams for a simple red Zinfandel from Amador or Lodi. The wines are fruit bombs with good tannins to complement the beef. I suggest one from Ravenswood or Rosenblum Cellars.

Preheat the oven to 200°F.

Slice each baguette lengthwise, without cutting all the way through, leaving the 2 sides attached. Lay the sliced baguettes, cut sides down, on a baking sheet and warm in the oven for 2 to 3 minutes.

In a large saucepan, heat the au jus over medium heat. When hot, drop the beef slices in the liquid and let them heat for about 1 minute. You do not want to cook the meat any further but simply heat it.

Remove the baguettes from the oven and put each one in a smaller pan, such as a pie plate, cut sides up. Turn on the broiler and adjust the heat source so that it is about 4 inches from the broiling pan.

Divide the sliced beef among the 4 baguettes. Lay the cheese over the sandwich to cover the meat and the edges of the bread. Slide the sandwiches, 1 at a time, under the broiler and heat for 15 to 20 seconds or until the cheese melts. Take care the bread does not burn.

Transfer each sandwich to a serving plate. Ladle au jus into 4 small cups and put a cup on each plate next to the sandwich for dipping. Garnish each sandwich with watercress and serve immediately.

MORTON'S TWO-FISTED BACON CHEESEBURGER

Matt Birk, a six-time All-Pro Center with the Minnesota Vikings, loves this big, juicy burger. Matt is also a Harvard graduate and a six-time Vikings Community Man of the Year. I call this the "two-fisted" burger because you really need both hands to manage it. As far as I am concerned, nothing beats a great hamburger with all the trimmings, and this one is fabulous. Use the best thick-cut bacon you can find—it is far superior to the more familiar thin-sliced break-fast bacon—and top the burger with horseradish cheddar cheese for extra zing. Four pounds of meat is a hefty amount, so if you must, stretch it out to serve eight. **SERVES 6**

4 pounds ground sirloin, see Note

4 large eggs

¾ cup tomato juice (we use Sacramento)

1 tablespoon kosher salt

1 teaspoon freshly ground black pepper

6 large hamburger buns

6 tablespoons (¾ stick) unsalted butter, softened

Seasoned salt

12 to 18 ounces sliced horseradish cheddar cheese, see Note

12 slices thick-cut bacon, cooked until crisp

Preheat the broiler.

In a large mixing bowl, break up the ground beef, add the egg and tomato juice, and season with the salt and pepper. Mix gently but thoroughly with your hands or a wooden spoon.

Divide the meat into 6 even portions and mold each into a patty about 1½ inches thick and 4½ inches in diameter. With a knife, make ⅛-inch-deep crisscrosses on top of each burger.

Brush the inside of each bun with butter and toast in the oven, in a toaster oven, or under the broiler, buttered sides up, until lightly browned. Remove the hot buns and season each buttered side with seasoned salt. Set aside.

Broil the burgers for 7 to 8 minutes on each side or until medium rare. Lay 3 slices of cheese on each burger and return to the broiler for about 30 seconds or until the cheese melts.

Sandwich the burgers in the buns and top each burger with 2 slices of bacon. Serve.

NOTE: We use a sirloin grind that is 20 percent fat, which may be hard to find. A grind that is 10 percent fat works well, too.

Horseradish cheddar cheese is sold at many cheese counters in supermarkets and delis.

SMOKED SALMON CLUB

For an impressive lunch dish, make a smoked salmon club sandwich. There is not much more to it than great bread, excellent smoked salmon, and good, fresh vegetables, but you don't need anything more for so appealing a meal. This sandwich used to be on our menu and we have guests who still ask for it. We may have to reinstate it sometime! **SERVES 2**

**3 large, thick slices home-style country bread,
    lightly toasted**

3 tablespoons Horseradish Sauce, opposite

2 large romaine lettuce leaves

4 ounces thinly sliced smoked salmon

2 tablespoons drained capers

4 very thin slices large beefsteak tomato

2 very thin slices large red onion

Spread 1 slice of toast with 1 tablespoon of the horseradish sauce. Lay a lettuce leaf on the sauce and then top with half the salmon, 2 of the capers, half the tomato slices, and 1 of the onion slices. Top with 1 slice of toast.

Repeat layering the remaining salmon, capers, tomato slices, and onion slice.

Spread another slice of toast with 1 tablespoon of the horseradish. Put the bread on top of the onion slice, horseradish side down. Gently press the sandwich closed.

Insert 4 toothpicks or decorative sandwich picks in the 4 quarters of the sandwich, about 1 inch from the crust.

Cut the sandwich on the diagonal between the picks into quarters. To do so, put your thumb on one side and your other fingers on the other side and with the knife under your hand, cut with a quick forward and downward motion. Repeat along the other diagonal. Serve 2 quarters for each serving.

Horseradish Sauce

5 tablespoons sour cream

3 tablespoons drained commercial
   horseradish

2 tablespoons mayonnaise

1 teaspoon Dijon mustard

⅛ teaspoon hot pepper sauce,
   such as Tabasco

⅛ teaspoon salt

Pinch of freshly ground white pepper

In a small bowl, mix together the sour cream, horseradish, mayonnaise, and mustard. Stir in the hot pepper sauce, salt, and pepper. Serve immediately or cover and refrigerate for up to 24 hours.

CRAB CAKE "BLT" SANDWICH

WITH DILL-CAPER SAUCE

Former New York Yankee All-Star second baseman and former manager of the New York Mets, Willie Randolph, is a good friend of Morton's. He and his wife dine regularly at our Hackensack, New Jersey, restaurant. Willie recently was our honoree at a Legends Event at our Morton's in Stamford, Connecticut.

For this delicious twist on a conventional BLT, we add a crab cake to the expected ingredients and turn a rather pedestrian sandwich into a feast! Many fish markets sell freshly made crab cakes and you can usually buy them frozen, too. The sauce is great on the sandwich and with other foods as well, such as salads, cold meats, and steamed vegetables. You only need about ½ cup for these sandwiches but our recipe makes a little more—you will be glad to have the leftovers! **SERVES 4**

SAUCE

¼ cup sour cream

¼ cup mayonnaise

1 teaspoon Dijon mustard

1½ teaspoons finely minced fresh dill

1½ teaspoons drained, finely minced capers

1 teaspoon fresh lemon juice

Pinch of Old Bay seasoning

SANDWICH

8 slices bacon

4 uncooked crab cakes

¾ cup Clarified Butter, page 227

8 slices home-style bread

8 leaves iceberg lettuce

8 slices tomato

WINE RECOMMENDATION
Our BLT calls for a spicy Malbec from Argentina, which will complement the bacon while still letting the crab shine through. I like a wine called Broquel from Mendoza. It is the high-end Malbec from Trapiche.

To make the sauce, in a small mixing bowl, whisk together the sour cream, mayonnaise, and mustard. Add the dill, capers, lemon juice, and Old Bay and whisk until fully incorporated. (Cover and refrigerate any extra sauce for up to 5 days.)

To make the sandwich: Preheat the oven to 500°F.

In a skillet, cook the bacon over medium heat until nearly crisp but not too firm, 2 to 3 minutes. Drain on paper towels and set aside.

Using a fork, gently flatten the crab cakes so that they will cover most of the bread.

Pour the clarified butter into a large, oven-safe skillet and arrange the crab cakes in the butter. Bake for about 3 minutes, turn the crab cakes, and cook for 2 minutes longer until heated through and browned.

Meanwhile, toast the bread in the toaster until golden brown. Spread about 1 tablespoon of sauce on each slice of bread.

Remove the crab cakes from the oven, lift them from the skillet, and set aside. Turn on the broiler.

Lay the bacon strips in the skillet and slide the skillet under the broiler. Broil for about 1 minute to reheat and crisp up.

Lay 2 leaves of lettuce on top of 4 slices of bread. Top each with a crab cake and 2 tomato slices. Crisscross the bacon strips on top of the tomatoes. Top with the remaining slices of bread, press down gently, cut in half, and serve.

RANCHER'S RIBEYE STEAK

STEAKHOUSE CLASSICS

James Patterson's Favorite
MORTON'S ROASTED PRIME RIB
WITH SHAVED FRESH HORSERADISH

——

Vernon Davis's Favorite
HERB-CRUSTED
DOUBLE PORTERHOUSE

——

John Riggin's Favorite
RANCHER'S RIBEYE STEAK

——

The Honorable Theodore B. Olson's Favorite
MORTON'S NEW YORK STRIP STEAK
WITH PARSLEY SAUCE

——

Val Kilmer's Favorite
FILET MIGNON
WITH A LIGHT GARLIC RUB

TENDERLOIN MEDALLIONS AL FORNO

——

Hannah Storm's Favorite
BONE-IN FILET

——

STEAK FLORENTINE

——

NEW YORK SIRLOIN STRIP ROAST
WITH THREE-PEPPERCORN SAUCE

——

SLICED TENDERLOIN TIPS WITH BACON
AND BLUE CHEESE

——

BLOODY MARY LONDON BROIL

Steak—great, truly amazing, only the best—always has been and always will be at the center of every Morton's restaurant, regardless of where in the world we open our doors. Steak is what most of our guests expect from us and is the reason they are so loyal. Steak is what people new to Morton's look forward to, and what makes them regulars.

Regardless of the other dishes we serve at the restaurants and that appear on the pages of this book, we remain true to our first love: steak. And who can blame us? Nothing tastes better!

In this chapter we offer steaks, along with a few other recipes that are so rich and beefy, we had to group them here.

To Cook a Steak

As it cooks, steak shrinks and loses moisture. That two-inch-thick strip steak you started with might measure only one and a half inches after it's cooked. Expect this.

At the restaurant, we cook our steaks over a very hot fire. Unless you have a very powerful grill or stove, you won't be able to attain these same temperatures and for this reason, we tested all our recipes in residential kitchens so that our cooking times and tests for doneness should work perfectly for you at home. Even so, I suggest you err on the side of undercooking rather than overcooking steaks and other meats. You can always toss the meat back on the grill if it's too undercooked, but there's no way to salvage a burned, gray steak.

Whether you cook steaks over hot coals, over gas elements in a gas grill, or under a broiler, the temperature should be hot enough to sear the meat the instant it hits the grill rack. We all love that sizzle! For most of our steak recipes, we instruct you to let the coals reach medium hot. Gas grills, which are a little cooler, should be turned up to high. Broilers, by definition, are very hot.

If your charcoal or gas grill has a thermometer, the heat is considered *hot* when the thermometer registers between 425° and 450°F. If you try to hold your open palm about four inches over the heat, you won't be able to hold it for longer than two seconds, and charcoal will be lightly covered with ash and glow red. For *medium-hot* temperatures, the thermometer will register between 375° and 425°F, you won't be able to hold your palm over the heat for longer than three seconds, and the coals will have a slightly thicker coating of gray ash covering the deep red glow. For *medium heat*, the thermometer will register between 325° and 375°F, you will be able to hold your palm over the heat for four seconds, and the gray ash will significantly cover the red, glowing coals.

The meat should be allowed to reach room temperature before it's cooked so that it will cook evenly and perfectly. We use nothing but our own seasoned salt on our steaks, a blend of salt and spices that we buy from a supplier who makes it to our specifications. This is not easy to duplicate in the home kitchen and so for the recipes here, we suggest you use our Morton's Seasoning Salt, which is available at www.mortons.com.

As you grill or broil the steak, its outside chars. The goal is to cook it just until the char is crispy and light. The meat's surface should not turn black and if it starts to, move the steak to a cooler part of the grill.

TIMING STEAK

We test our steaks for doneness by time and by feel. Both are subjective. Timing will vary from broiler to broiler and grill to grill, which is why we suggest you view the cooking times in our recipes as guides, not absolutes. When a steak is on the grill or under the broiler, turn it only once and use tongs.

Not all cuts of meat feel exactly the same but, as they cook, all reach different degrees of doneness in similar ways. If you press lightly on a raw strip steak or T-bone, it will feel firmer than a raw filet mignon. As these cuts cook, each will feel different as it reaches each stage of doneness, but the principles will be the same.

During cooking, the naturally occurring fat in the steak, called marbling, softens and much of it melts. The fatty acids release pleasing aromatic compounds as well as wonderful flavor compounds that are only experienced in beef. This explains why a well-marbled steak will give you better flavor than one that is too lean. Marbling also ensures juiciness.

To understand our timing methods and tests for doneness, follow these guidelines:

Test steak doneness by feel. You may have seen chefs pressing their fingers into meat on the grill. To understand what they are doing, hold your hand out, palm up, and follow these guidelines:

FOR RARE MEAT: Poke the pad at the base of the thumb. If the meat feels like this, it's ready.

FOR MEDIUM-RARE MEAT: Press the area of your palm between the thumb pad and the center of the palm. If the meat feels like this, it's ready.

FOR MEDIUM MEAT: Press the middle of your palm. If the meat feels like this, it's ready.

FOR WELL-DONE MEAT: Press the base of the pinkie. If the meat feels like this, it's ready.

This is not a foolproof method, but it is a good place to start. Different cuts of meat will feel different from one another, but *the degree* of difference between rare and medium-rare, and so on, will be the same.

There are other ways to determine doneness. For example, if you like medium-rare meat, a bone-in steak is done when the meat is still firmly attached to the bone. When the meat on a porterhouse or T-bone starts to pull away from the bone, it is past medium-rare and on its way to medium.

Watch the juices that naturally escape from the meat. The steak won't release much juice when the meat in the middle is still red, but when it starts to turn pink inside, it will. If you notice small pockets of juice collecting on the meat and they look a little white, you can be sure the meat inside is medium.

Many home cooks like to use instant-read thermometers to determine when the beef is done. We don't recommend it because we don't like to puncture our steaks until it's time to take knife and fork to them, but we recognize this might make it easier for the novice steak cook—at least until he or she gets the hang of the other tests. Here are the recommended temperatures for doneness; the USDA-approved temperatures are the higher ones. The USDA has no temperature recommendations for rare meat. We consider meat rare when it is between 125° and 130°F.

MEDIUM-RARE: 135° to 145°F

MEDIUM: 145° to 150°F

WELL-DONE: 150° to 165°F

(These temperatures apply to lamb as well.)

When the steak is cooked, let it rest on a cutting board or platter to give the juices an opportunity to redistribute throughout the meat. There is no need to cover the meat as it rests. Follow our recommendation for the time needed for resting.

✍ CELEBRITY CLIP ✍

PROFESSIONAL ATHLETES, who are in essence business travelers, are huge fans of the steaks and seafood at Morton's. LeBron James dines regularly with us wherever he is on the road: New York City, New Orleans, and Macau, China, are a few cities where LeBron has visited Morton's, and of course at his local Cleveland location. Derek Jeter and some of his longtime Yankees teammates make it a ritual every year, when they go on their West Coast road trip to Northern California, to dine at Morton's in the Union Square area of San Francisco. Tiger Woods loves our Orlando Morton's, and Peyton Manning frequents his hometown team's Indianapolis location. And in one week, the men who oversee their respective sports leagues were all seen at Morton's: MLB commissioner Bud Selig, NFL commissioner Roger Goodell, NHL commissioner Gary Bettman, and former MLB commissioner Peter Ueberroth came in to try the best steak anywhere! ✍

MORTON'S ROASTED PRIME RIB

WITH SHAVED FRESH HORSERADISH

James Patterson is an accomplished author who holds the record for being on the New York Times *bestseller list thirty-nine times! We are big fans of his books, and we love that he frequently mentions us in many of his novels, as well as the fact that he dines with us frequently.*

When you cook a prime rib roast, be sure to let the meat sit at room temperature for about 1 hour; otherwise it won't cook evenly. Put the roast on a rack in a roasting pan—do not set the roast in the bottom of the pan and do not let it overcook. I like to shave fresh horseradish over it for a spectacular presentation. **SERVES 10 TO 12**

One 12- to 14-pound seven-rib aged prime rib
½ cup seasoned salt

1 pound fresh horseradish, well washed
¾ cup Au Jus, page 229, optional

COCKTAIL RECOMMENDATION
Sazerac, page 19.

A day before cooking the roast, season it on all sides with the seasoned salt. Transfer the roast to a pan. Cover with aluminum foil and refrigerate overnight.

Position the oven rack in the lowest position possible and preheat the oven to 325°F. Remove the roast from the refrigerator about 1 hour before roasting and allow to come to room temperature.

Set a rack in a large roasting pan and set the roast on the rack. Roast for 2½ to 3 hours for medium-rare, or until the roast reaches the desired degree of doneness. The meat will be more well-done at the ends and rarer in the center.

Lift the roast from the pan and set it on a cutting board. Loosely tent the roast with aluminum foil to keep it warm and let the meat rest at room temperature for 15 to 20 minutes.

Using a vegetable peeler, peel the horseradish root.

Remove the lip of the roast—the portion on top of the bones in front of the eye—and discard. Starting with the small end, carve the roast into thick pieces. To serve, spoon some of the au jus onto a plate, if desired. Put a slice of meat on top of the sauce.

Using the vegetable peeler, shave 4 to 5 thin slices of horseradish on top of each serving. The horseradish shavings should be as long, thin, and dramatic looking as you can make them. Serve with more jus spooned over the meat, if desired.

HERB-CRUSTED DOUBLE PORTERHOUSE

Vernon Davis, starting tight end for the San Francisco 49ers, is a big fan of our steaks, especially the porterhouse. In a recent issue of San Jose *magazine, he was asked about his favorite meal. He replied it was the porterhouse at Morton's.*

This is a cut of meat you will have to special-order. It's huge and is quite popular at the restaurant. Every now and then we have guests who bet with each other that they can't eat a whole steak—and usually they cannot! We slice it at the table and there is more than enough for four hungry guys. When you take it from the oven, let it rest for about 10 minutes and then slice it in front of your guests. They will be impressed, and very satisfied. Of course, you could just as easily serve four 12-ounce porterhouse steaks, which are easier for the home cook to find and will taste just as good.

SERVES 4

¼ cup chopped fresh basil

¼ cup chopped fresh sage

2 tablespoons chopped fresh rosemary

2 tablespoons minced fresh thyme

1 tablespoon kosher salt

1 tablespoon freshly ground black pepper

3 cloves garlic, minced

2 tablespoons extra-virgin olive oil

One 48-ounce porterhouse, 2½ to 3 inches
   thick, or four 12-ounce porterhouse steaks

Vegetable oil cooking spray

Seasoned salt

2 tablespoons Au Jus, page 229, optional

WINE RECOMMENDATION

This presentation is similar to that of dishes found in the Tuscany region of Italy, and because both the filet and strip are on the porterhouse, you want to choose a wine that does not over- or underwhelm either. Again, Sangiovese is good choice. I would go with a highly tannic Brunello from Biondi-Santi or a Super Tuscan, IGT like Tignanello. While pricey, these wines will be the most memorable with this dish.

In a small bowl, mix together the basil, sage, rosemary, thyme, salt, and pepper. Add the garlic and oil and stir to form a paste. You will have about 1 cup of paste.

Rub the paste on both sides of the steak. Let the steak sit at room temperature for about 30 minutes.

Meanwhile, prepare a charcoal or gas grill or preheat the broiler and position a rack 4 inches from the heating element. Before igniting the grill, lightly spray the grill rack with cooking spray. The coals should be medium-hot for the charcoal grill. The burners should be on high for the gas grill.

recipe continues on page 102

If using a charcoal or gas grill, preheat the oven to 500°F. If your oven will heat to 550°F, do so.

Grill or broil the steak for about 5 minutes. Turn, using tongs, and grill the other side for about 5 minutes, just long enough to sear both sides so that the herb rub adheres to the meat and starts to turn crispy. Remove from the grill or broiler and transfer to a roasting pan.

If you used a broiler, heat the oven to 500°F. If your oven will heat to 550°F, do so.

Roast the steak in the oven for 35 to 40 minutes for medium-rare or the desired degree of doneness.

Put the steak on a cutting board and let it rest for 10 to 12 minutes. Slice the steak ¼ inch thick, arrange on a serving platter, and spoon au jus over the slices, if desired.

MORTON'S-SIZE STEAK DINNER MENU

MORTON'S FIVE-ONION SOUP, PAGE 72

MORTON'S CENTER-CUT ICEBERG SALAD, PAGE 54

HERB-CRUSTED DOUBLE PORTERHOUSE, PAGE 100

TWICE-BAKED POTATOES, PAGE 199

CRÈME BRÛLÉE, PAGE 217

HEAVENLY COSMOPOLITAN, PAGE 15

RANCHER'S RIBEYE STEAK

Super Bowl Washington Redskins' running back, John Riggins, dines at our D.C.-area Morton's and the ribeye is his #1 entrée. Everyone has heard of ribeyes, but people tend to order sirloin or strip rather than these tasty cuts. This is a shame because the ribye is cut from the prime rib section and is a rich-tasting piece of beef, and nearly as tender as steaks from the short loin. Ribeyes should be well marbled and may or may not have a noticeable nugget of creamy fat embedded in the meat. When a ribeye is sold with its bone, it's called a bone-in rib steak—and is delicious. Apply our simple rancher's rub generously, working it into the meat with your fingers. **SERVES 6**

½ cup ancho chile powder or pure chile powder

½ cup mild paprika

¼ cup kosher salt

¼ cup sugar

1 teaspoon freshly ground black pepper

Six 16-ounce aged ribeye steaks, each about 1½ inches thick

4¾ cups flavorless vegetable oil, such as canola or safflower oil

6 tablespoons Au Jus, page 229, optional

WINE RECOMMENDATION
Ribeye and chile powder. Delicious! A perfect wine match is a high-octane Australian Shiraz. Any of the Shirazes from Two Hands (Bella's Garden is my favorite) would be divine with this dish. Almost like drinking spicy chocolate, they complement the fat in the ribeye and stand up to the chile and other spices.

In a mixing bowl, stir together the chile powder, paprika, salt, sugar, and pepper. Transfer to a large, shallow glass or ceramic pan. You will have about 1½ cups of rancher's rub.

Remove the steaks from the refrigerator about 40 minutes before cooking. Lay the steaks, 1 at a time, in the dish and press the rancher's rub into each side of the steaks to cover completely. Remove the steaks and lightly pound each 4 to 5 times on both sides with a meat mallet or small heavy skillet to soften but not flatten more than a little. Discard any remaining seasoning in the pan. Set aside to marinate at room temperature for 35 minutes.

Prepare a charcoal or gas grill or preheat the broiler and position a rack 4 inches from the heating element. The coals should be medium-hot for the charcoal grill. The burners should be on high for the gas grill.

Grill or broil for about 8 minutes. Turn using tongs and cook the other side for 8 to 9 minutes for medium-rare, or until desired degree of doneness.

To serve, spoon some of the au jus over the steaks, if desired.

MORTON'S NEW YORK STRIP STEAK

WITH PARSLEY SAUCE

The Honorable Theodore B. Olson really enjoys our New York Strip Steak. He's a regular at our Washington, D.C., Morton's on Connecticut Avenue, dining with us two or three times a week, often with his wife, Lady Booth Olson.

Our guests, who also call this tender steak New York sirloin or New York steak, absolutely love this cut. Despite these nomenclatures, the steak does not have to be eaten in the Big Apple to be enjoyed, and when topped with a fresh-tasting, easy-to-make parsley sauce, it's better than ever. Avoid strip steaks with an obvious vein running through the meat, as the vein tends to make the meat curl up when cooking. **SERVES 6**

STEAK

**Three 20-ounce aged New York strip steaks,
each about 2 inches thick**

Vegetable oil cooking spray

1 tablespoon seasoned salt

SAUCE

**1 bunch flat-leaf parsley, chopped, large stems
discarded**

8 cloves garlic, chopped

½ cup minced white onion

¼ cup white vinegar

1 medium jalapeño pepper, seeded and minced

2 teaspoons chopped fresh oregano

1 teaspoon kosher salt

½ teaspoon freshly ground black pepper

1 cup extra-virgin olive oil

BEER RECOMMENDATION

Considering the spiciness of the sauce, it's a good idea to drink beer with this dish—most wines would be lost with these competing flavors. Try a beer made in a dark style with a high hops content. I recommend Samuel Smith Oatmeal Stout, a full, creamy brew with enough body to truly complement the richness of the beef and the complexity of the sauce.

To cook the steaks: Remove the steaks from the refrigerator and let them rest at room temperature for 30 minutes.

Meanwhile, make the sauce: In the bowl of a food processor fitted with a metal blade, mix together the parsley, garlic, onion, vinegar, ¼ cup water, the jalapeño, oregano, salt, and pepper. Pulse 2 to 3 times until mixed.

With the motor running, add the olive oil in a steady stream through the feed tube. Mix only until the sauce is still slightly coarse in texture. You will have about 2½ cups of sauce. Set aside until serving.

To prepare a charcoal or gas grill, lightly spray the grill rack with cooking spray. Or pre-heat the broiler and position a rack 4 inches from the heating element. The coals should be medium-hot for the charcoal grill. The burners should be on high for the gas grill.

Season the steaks lightly on both sides with the seasoned salt. Grill or broil for 10 minutes. Turn using tongs and cook the other side for 9 to 11 minutes for medium-rare, or until desired degree of doneness.

To serve, spoon some of the sauce over the steaks and pass the rest on the side.

✎ CELEBRITY CLIP ✎

IN THE COLDEST MONTHS of fall and winter, our restaurants around the world are something of a haven for musicians, actors, athletes, politicians, and even royalty—all of whom seem to be in search of the same thing: an unforgettable steakhouse dining experience. In New York a few years ago during United Nations week, then-president of France, Jacques Chirac, brought in a group of twenty political leaders and clearly enjoyed, among other items, our French fries. In Singapore we were visited by another statesman, the former prime minister of Japan, Junichiro Koizumi. Political odd couple Mary Matalin and James Carville dined together in Palm Desert, California, and also are seen regularly at our restaurant in Arlington, Virginia. Prince Andrew, the Duke of York, hosted a dinner at the Phoenix Morton's with Arizona governor Janet Napolitano and several Phoenix-based CEOs. The royal party enjoyed filet mignon and the New York strip. ✎

FILET MIGNON
with Light Garlic Rub

I like to rub a light seasoning mix on a good filet. The meat does not need much to enhance its buttery texture and mild flavor, but a little garlic and dash of cayenne provides just enough zip to make you sit up and smack your lips! When you cook a filet mignon, take care not to overcook it. For a steak it is lean, and because of this does not have much fat to protect it from the heat. This is our customers' favorite cut. It's tender, buttery, and juicy, although it lacks the full-bodied beef flavor some of the other cuts have. Filet mignon is cut from the tenderloin. It's also the favorite dish of Hollywood movie star Val Kilmer, who we often see at our Los Angeles area restaurants. **SERVES 6**

4 teaspoons granulated garlic

2 teaspoons kosher salt

2 teaspoons freshly ground black pepper

½ teaspoon cayenne pepper

Six 14-ounce filet mignons, each 2 to 2½ inches thick

Vegetable oil cooking spray

6 tablespoons Au Jus, page 229, optional

COCKTAIL SUGGESTION
Iced Vodka with Sirloin Garnish, page 12

To make the rub: Combine the garlic, salt, black pepper, and cayenne pepper.

To prepare the steaks: Remove the steaks from the refrigerator, rub them on both sides with the rub, and let them rest at room temperature for 30 minutes.

Prepare a charcoal or gas grill or preheat the broiler and position a rack 4 inches from the heating element. Lightly spray the grill rack with cooking spray. The coals should be medium-hot for the charcoal grill. If using a gas grill, put the burners on high.

If using a grill, grill the filets for about 8 minutes. Turn and grill for 6 to 8 minutes for medium-rare or longer until desired degree of doneness. If using the broiler, broil for 9 minutes. Turn and broil for 8 to 10 minutes for medium-rare or longer until the desired degree of doneness.

Serve with the au jus spooned over the steaks, if desired.

TENDERLOIN MEDALLIONS AL FORNO

This has been a popular item on our lunch menu for some time. It's a small medallion of beef flavored with garlic and Parmesan and served with an indulgent creamy pasta. You can omit the pasta for a lighter meal. Either way, this looks, smells, and tastes great. **SERVES 2**

Eight 2-ounce tenderloin medallions

About 5 ounces dried spinach fettuccine

Seasoned salt

¼ cup Clarified Butter, page 227

4 tablespoons (½ stick) unsalted butter

½ cup heavy cream

¼ cup freshly grated Parmesan cheese

¼ cup melted Garlic Butter, page 110

WINE RECOMMENDATION
A Cabernet-based wine is a pleasing companion for this dish and a super Tuscan blend fits the bill. The hints of oak and spices bring out the underlying flavors of the food, while the tannins in the wine support the creaminess without overpowering the delicate flavors. Try Banfi Summus, Tuscany. A rich and complex Italian wine such as a Barolo works well, too. We suggest Marchesi di Barolo Cannubi, from Piedmont.

Remove the medallions from the refrigerator and let them rest at room temperature for 30 to 60 minutes.

Preheat the broiler.

Cook the fettuccine according to the package instructions until al dente. Drain and set aside, covered, to keep warm.

Season the medallions on both sides with seasoned salt.

In a sauté pan, heat the clarified butter over medium-high heat and when hot, sauté the medallions for 1½ to 2 minutes on each side for medium-rare. Set aside.

Heat another sauté pan over medium heat and when hot, melt the butter. Add the cream, cook for about 1 minute to warm it up, and then add the cooked pasta. Mix thoroughly and cook for 1 to 2 minutes or until the pasta is nicely coated with cream and the sauce reduces slightly. Sprinkle half of the Parmesan over the pasta and toss to mix. Cover to keep warm.

Arrange the medallions on a broiler tray or oven-safe serving dish and ladle a little garlic butter over each medallion. Sprinkle half of the remaining cheese over the medallions. Broil for 20 to 30 seconds or until the cheese turns golden brown. Do not overcook. Serve the medallions alongside the warm pasta, which should be sprinkled with the remaining cheese.

GARLIC BUTTER

You will love our garlic butter, once you get in the habit of making it. Add it to plain vegetables, potatoes, pasta, or rice and don't add another seasoning. We love it with mushrooms. Try it with our mashed potatoes for garlic mashed potatoes. You can make a lot at once—you could easily double this recipe—and keep it in the freezer for a month or two. Knowing it's right there makes home cooking so much easier. Don't be put off by the anchovies; they simply provide a depth of saltiness you can't get any other way. **MAKES ABOUT 1¼ CUPS**

1 generous tablespoon chopped garlic

1 tablespoon chopped shallot

1 teaspoon chopped rinsed and drained anchovies (1 to 2 fillets)

About ½ cup chopped fresh flat-leaf parsley leaves (about ¼ bunch)

10 tablespoons (1½ sticks) unsalted butter, softened

¾ teaspoon Pernod liqueur

1 teaspoon coarse salt

½ teaspoon freshly ground white pepper

In the bowl of a food processor fitted with the metal blade, pulse the garlic, shallot, anchovies, and parsley until finely chopped.

In the bowl of an electric mixer fitted with the paddle attachment and set on medium speed, beat the butter for 1 minute. Scrape the garlic mixture into the butter and beat for another minute or so until thoroughly combined. Reduce the speed to low. Add the Pernod, salt, and pepper and beat to combine. Increase the speed to high and mix for 2 minutes, or until the butter is smooth, fluffy, and light. Scrape down the sides of the bowl with a rubber spatula. Mix for 2 more minutes at high speed.

Use immediately or transfer to an airtight container. Refrigerate for up to 5 days, or wrap well and freeze for up to 2 months.

BONE-IN FILET

We included this recipe in the book after some debate, but in the end we decided it was so delicious and so appealing, we had to have it. It's not easy to find bone-in filet. Without question, you will have to special order it and even then some butchers will not be able to get it. We even have a hard time finding enough to stock all our restaurants, but when we have it, our guests love it. The bone gives the filet more flavor than it ordinarily has, as most filet is more about its buttery texture than taste. Hannah Storm of ESPN calls this beef entrée her favorite, and she's a favorite of ours as well, as we've previously honored her as a "Legend" at the annual fundraiser we host at our Morton's in Stamford, Connecticut. **SERVES 6**

Six 16-ounce bone-in filet steaks, each about 2 inches thick
Vegetable oil cooking spray

Seasoned salt
6 tablespoons Au Jus, page 229, optional

Remove the steaks from the refrigerator and let them rest at room temperature for 30 to 60 minutes.

Meanwhile, prepare a charcoal or gas grill or preheat the broiler and position a rack 4 inches from the heating element. Before igniting the grill, lightly spray the grill rack with cooking spray. The coals should be medium-hot for the charcoal grill. The burners should be on high for the gas grill.

Season the steaks with seasoned salt on both sides.

If using a charcoal or gas grill, grill the meat for 6 minutes. Turn, using tongs, and grill the other side for 6 to 7 minutes for medium-rare, or until the desired degree of doneness. (During grilling, rotate the meat so that the bone does not burn.) If using the broiler, broil 4 inches from the heat source for about 7 minutes. Turn, using tongs, and broil the other side for about 7 minutes for medium-rare or until the desired degree of doneness.

Transfer the steaks to a cutting board and let them rest for 2 to 3 minutes. Serve with the au jus spooned over each one, if desired.

STEAK FLORENTINE

These tasty steaks are served on a bed of spinach, which earns them their name. Both round and butt steaks are full of flavor, and they are so well appreciated all across America that we think of them as "American cuts." They are chewier than sirloin or tenderloin but full of great beef flavor. If you can find prime beef, buy it, but choice will do just fine here. **SERVES 2**

Two 10-ounce round or butt steaks, each about 1 inch thick

1½ tablespoons unsalted butter

1 tablespoon minced shallot (1 small shallot)

1 pound fresh spinach, stemmed

1 tablespoon minced garlic

Kosher salt and freshly ground black pepper

1 tablespoon olive oil

2 tablespoons freshly grated Parmesan cheese

WINE RECOMMENDATION

Pinotage wine from New Zealand has medium body with low tannin and high acidity, making it a good match for both the mildly bitter spinach and the Parmesan cheese. Try Te Awa Winery's Pinotage from Hawkes Bay, New Zealand.

Rosso di Montalcino is the little brother to Brunello di Montalcino and will complement this dish nicely. It is a fruity, low-tannin wine that balances the bitter spinach but does not overpower the lean meat. We recommend Banfi Rosso di Montalcino from Tuscany.

Remove the steaks from the refrigerator and let them rest at room temperature for 30 to 60 minutes.

Preheat the oven to 400°F.

In a large sauté pan, melt 1 tablespoon of the butter over medium heat and when hot, add the shallots and cook for 1 to 2 minutes or until soft. Add the spinach to the pan and cook for 3 to 4 minutes, stirring, or until the spinach just wilts. Do not let it get too limp. Remove the pan from the heat, cover to keep warm, and set aside.

In a small sauté pan, heat the remaining ½ tablespoon butter over medium-low heat and cook the garlic for 2 to 3 minutes or until it begins to brown. Set aside.

Lightly sprinkle the steaks with salt and pepper.

In another large sauté pan, heat the olive oil over medium-high heat and when very hot, sear the steaks for about 2 minutes on each side. Transfer the steaks to a roasting pan and roast for 3 to 4 minutes or until barely medium-rare.

Remove the steaks from the oven and turn on the broiler.

Drain the liquid from the spinach and spread the spinach in a broiler pan. Set the steaks on top of the spinach and then top each steak with the garlic and butter. Sprinkle a tablespoon of cheese over each steak and broil for 1 to 2 minutes or until the cheese melts and is lightly browned. Let the steak rest for 5 to 10 minutes. Divide between 2 plates.

NEW YORK SIRLOIN STRIP ROAST
WITH THREE-PEPPERCORN SAUCE

When you buy a sirloin strip roast, ask the butcher to remove its vein, which will make it very easy to slice the meat. We recommend slicing it thin and serving it with the peppercorn sauce in this recipe, but you may prefer horseradish Both are great. **SERVES 4 TO 6**

One 3½- to 4-pound center-cut boneless
   New York sirloin strip roast
Kosher salt and freshly ground black pepper
½ tablespoon unsalted butter
2 tablespoons coarsely cracked three-
   peppercorn mix

1 tablespoon finely chopped shallot
   (1 small shallot)
1 small clove garlic, finely chopped
¼ cup Cognac
1½ cups reconstituted store-bought
   demi-glace, see Note page 117
1 cup heavy cream

WINE RECOMMENDATION
The spicy cinnamon flavors and low tannins of Australian Shiraz balance nicely with the heat of the peppercorn mix. The cedar flavor brings out the richness of the Cognac and heavy cream sauce. We recommend Penfolds Bin 28, Kalimna Shiraz, from McLaren Vale, South Australia, and various labels from the Barossa Valley in South Australia.

A Southern Rhône blend pairs with this just as nicely as does the Shiraz. We suggest Châteauneuf-du-Pape or Châteauneuf-du-Pape Vieux Télégraphe.

Remove the roast from the refrigerator and let it rest at room temperature for 30 to 60 minutes.

Preheat the oven to 400°F.

Season the roast on all sides with salt and pepper and transfer to a roasting pan. Roast for 45 to 55 minutes for medium-rare. Remove from the oven and let the roast rest on a cutting board for 10 to 15 minutes before slicing.

In a small saucepan, melt the butter over medium heat. Add the peppercorns, shallot, and garlic and cook for about 2 minutes or until the shallot softens.

Stir the Cognac into the sauce and simmer for about 2 minutes or until nearly all the liquid evaporates.

Add the demi-glace and cream, bring to a simmer, and cook for 15 to 20 minutes or until the sauce reduces to about 1 cup. Season to taste with salt and pepper.

Slice the roast into thin slices and serve with the sauce passed on the side.

SLICED TENDERLOIN TIPS
WITH BACON AND BLUE CHEESE

The applewood-smoked bacon goes splendidly with the blue cheese, as you will see with the first bite. If you can't find applewood-smoked bacon, use any high-quality, thick-cut bacon. If you want to make this for more people, the recipe doubles or triples very nicely. **SERVES 2**

12 ounces tenderloin tips (2 to 3 pieces), see Note

2 slices thick-cut applewood-smoked bacon or other thick-cut bacon, cut into ½-inch-thick pieces

1 large shallot, sliced (⅓ to ½ cup)

2 tablespoons red wine

1 plum tomato, diced

½ cup reconstituted store-bought veal demi-glace, see Note

Kosher salt and freshly ground black pepper

1 tablespoon cooking oil

¼ cup crumbled blue cheese (1 ounce)

WINE RECOMMENDATION
The salt in the bacon balances the acidity and tannin in an American Cabernet Sauvignon, and the richness of the steak, cheese, and bacon bring out the wine's depth. Try Parducci Cabernet Sauvignon from Mendocino, California.

COCKTAIL RECOMMENDATION
A ten-year-old Laphroaig scotch, from Islay, Scotland.

Remove the tenderloin tips from the refrigerator and let them rest at room temperature for 30 to 60 minutes.

Preheat the oven to 325°F.

In a skillet set over medium heat, sauté the bacon until nearly crisp. Remove from the pan and drain on paper towels.

Add the shallot to the skillet and sauté, stirring frequently, for 2 to 3 minutes or until softened and starting to brown. Add the wine and tomato and cook for 1 to 2 minutes or until the wine evaporates.

Add the demi-glace and half of the drained bacon, raise the heat to high, and cook for 3 to 4 minutes, stirring occasionally or until reduced to a thick consistency and there is about ½ cup of chunky sauce. Season to taste with salt and pepper. Set aside.

Lightly sprinkle salt and pepper over the meat.

Heat the oil in a medium sauté pan set over high heat, add the meat, and cook for about 1 minute on each side or until well browned. Brown the meat a piece or two at a time so as not to crowd the pan. Transfer to a rimmed baking sheet or shallow roasting pan and bake for about 4 minutes for medium-rare. Transfer to a cutting board and let rest for 10 minutes.

Turn on the broiler.

Slice the meat crosswise into ½-inch-thick slices and arrange on the baking sheet. Sprinkle the blue cheese over the meat and broil for about 1 minute or until the cheese melts.

Spoon the sauce over each of 2 serving plates. Set the meat on top of the sauce and serve, garnished with the remaining bacon.

NOTE: Tenderloin tips, also called tails, are the tapering end of the filet mignon, or tenderloin. When the tails, or tips, are removed the remaining center of the tenderloin is called a chateaubriand.

You can buy veal demi-glace in a small container, usually about 1½ ounces, in specialty food stores, select supermarkets, and even some discount food clubs. We like More Than Gourmet Demi-Glace Gold. To find a convenient location where it's sold or to order it online, go to www.morethangourmet.com.

BLOODY MARY LONDON BROIL

I developed this recipe almost by accident. I planned to cook a flank steak and was thinking about how I would marinate it to tenderize it. I saw a bottle of spicy Bloody Mary mix in the refrigerator and so gave it a try. It was phenomenal. Use regular Bloody Mary mix if you prefer. **SERVES 3 TO 4**

1 quart (4 cups) regular or spicy Bloody Mary mix

One 1½- to 2-pound flank steak

Vegetable oil cooking spray

Horseradish Sauce, page 89, for serving

WINE RECOMMENDATION
The earthy fruitiness of the Zinfandel grape from California matches delightfully with the grilled lean meat and the savory spices of the Bloody Mary mix. We like Ridge York Creek Zinfandel from Napa, California.

COCKTAIL RECOMMENDATION
Morton's Bloody Mary, page 23

In a glass or rigid plastic dish large enough to hold the steak easily or in a sealable plastic bag, pour the Bloody Mary mix over the steak. Cover or zip the bag closed and refrigerate for at least 4 hours and up to 6 hours.

Lift the meat from the marinade and let most of it drip off the meat. Discard the marinade. Let the meat sit at room temperature for about 30 minutes.

Meanwhile, prepare a charcoal or gas grill or preheat the broiler and position a rack 4 inches from the heating element. Before igniting the grill, lightly spray the grill rack with cooking spray. The coals should be medium-hot for the charcoal grill. The burners should be on high for the gas grill.

If using a charcoal or gas grill, grill the meat for 7 minutes. Turn, using tongs, and grill the other side for 6 to 7 minutes for medium-rare, or until the desired degree of doneness. If using the broiler, broil 4 inches from the heat source for about 7 minutes. Turn, using tongs, and broil the other side for about 8 minutes for medium-rare or until the desired degree of doneness.

Transfer the meat to a cutting board and let it rest for 8 to 10 minutes. Slice the steak across the grain into ½-inch-thick slices. Serve with horseradish sauce on the side.

MORTON'S SHORT RIBS

MORE MAIN-COURSE EVENTS

ROASTED VEAL CHOPS

———

KLAUS'S VEAL WITH MUSHROOMS
AND SPAETZLE

———

VEAL SALTIMBOCCA

———

CALVES' LIVER WITH APPLES, ONIONS,
AND BACON

———

ROASTED VEAL SHANKS

———

STEAK BENEDICT

———

MORTON'S MEATLOAF

———

COLORADO BEEF BRISKET

———

KLAUS'S CORNED BEEF HASH

———

MORTON'S CHOPPED STEAK

———

MORTON'S SHORT RIBS

———

HERB-CRUSTED LAMB LOIN

———

RACK OF LAMB WELLINGTON

———

LAMB CHOPS PICCATA

———

STUFFED PORK CHOPS

———

TUSCAN PORK CHOPS

———

OLD-FASHIONED ROASTED PORK LOIN

———

BARBECUED BABY BACK RIBS

———

OLD-FASHIONED ROASTED CHICKEN

———

STUFFED CHICKEN BREASTS

———

SAUTÉED DUCK BREASTS WITH PORT
AND GARLIC

ROASTED VEAL CHOPS

We suggest long-boned veal chops because they create a dramatic presentation; if your butcher can order them for you, your guests will be mightily impressed. If you cannot get them, don't avoid the recipe. It's just as tasty with veal chops without the long bones. This simple, rustic dish is a perfect example of the best of French country cooking. The gorgeous sauce, with the thick-cut mushrooms, is equally good with chicken and pork. **SERVES 4**

4 veal chops (each 16 to 20 ounces), with 5-inch-long bones, see Note

1 tablespoon unsalted butter

3 tablespoons minced shallots (2 to 3 small shallots)

1 tablespoon minced garlic

8 ounces shiitake mushrooms, stemmed and sliced ½ inch thick (about 3 cups)

8 ounces cremini mushrooms, sliced ½ inch thick (about 3 cups)

8 ounces white mushrooms, sliced ½ inch thick (about 3 cups)

¾ cup dry white wine

3 cups reconstituted store-bought veal demi-glace, see Note, page 117

4 large plum tomatoes, peeled, seeded, and chopped into ¼-inch dice (about 1 cup), see Note

Kosher salt and freshly ground black pepper

1 tablespoon extra-virgin olive oil

Chopped fresh flat-leaf parsley, for serving

Remove the veal chops from the refrigerator and let them rest at room temperature for 30 to 60 minutes.

Preheat the oven to 400°F.

In a large sauté pan, melt the butter over medium heat and when hot, add the shallots and garlic and cook for about 2 minutes or until soft. Add the mushrooms and cover the pan. Let the mushrooms cook for about 5 minutes or until they begin to soften and release their moisture. Add the wine, raise the heat to medium-high, and when the liquid boils, cook for about 5 minutes until the liquid reduces by about three quarters.

Add the demi-glace, bring to a simmer, and cook for about 15 minutes, stirring occasionally, or until the flavors blend and the demi-glace is well incorporated. Stir in the tomatoes and season with salt and pepper. You will have about 4 cups of sauce. Turn the heat down to low and cover to keep the sauce warm.

Lightly season the veal chops with salt and pepper.

recipe continues on page 124

In a large sauté pan, heat the oil until hot. Brown the veal chops for about 2 minutes on each side. Using tongs, brown the sides of the chops, too. You will have to do this in batches. Transfer the browned chops to a roasting pan.

Roast the chops for 18 to 20 minutes or until medium. Transfer them to a cutting board and let them rest for 4 to 5 minutes. Serve with the sauce spooned over them and garnished with parsley.

NOTE: We serve these veal chops with long frenched bones (bones from which all meat and fat has been removed). You may be able to buy them from a high-quality butcher shop, although you probably will have to special order them. If you can't find veal chops with long bones, the dish is still delicious. The chops will weigh less, from 12 to 16 ounces each.

The easiest way to peel the tomatoes is to blanch them first. Bring a pot of water to a boil and submerge the tomatoes in it for 45 to 60 seconds. Remove them with a slotted spoon and transfer them immediately to a bowl filled with ice water. As soon as they cool, the skins will slip off. You hardly need a knife. To seed the tomatoes, cut them in half and hold them, cut side down, over a plate or bowl. Gently squeeze the tomato halves so that the seeds fall out.

✎ CELEBRITY CLIP ✎

We opened our third Asia Morton's in Macau in the late summer of 2007, at the Venetian Resort Hotel and Casino on the world-famous Cotai Strip. It has become a hot spot for American celebrities traveling in that part of the world. While in town for a basketball exhibition, NBA megastar LeBron James came in for a visit, and soon after, during a three-match exhibition, tennis stars Roger Federer and Pete Sampras celebrated together after their final match. Federer had the single-cut filet, medium-well, and Sampras volleyed with the rib-eye steak cooked medium-rare. It was a family affair after Celine Dion's concert at the Venetian when she and her husband-manager René Angélil dined with their son and Celine's sister and mother. Celine enjoyed her Cajun rib-eye and French fries so much that following her meal, she asked to meet with Chef See Tok to thank him for preparing such a wonderful meal. ✎

KLAUS'S VEAL
WITH MUSHROOMS AND SPAETZLE

Just about everyone in Switzerland knows how to make a version of this dish, and when I lived there, it quickly became a great personal favorite. I make it often for my American friends and everyone loves it. The spaetzle is just perfect for soaking up the sauce, although you can substitute egg noodles. **SERVES 4**

2 pounds veal, thinly sliced and cut into
   1-inch-wide strips
1 tablespoon unsalted butter
2 tablespoons finely chopped shallots
   (2 small shallots)
4 ounces medium white or shiitake
   mushrooms, thinly sliced (about 1½ cups)
¼ cup dry white wine
2 tablespoons reconstituted store-bought veal
   demi-glace, see Note, page 117

1 tablespoon cornstarch
1 cup heavy cream
Salt and freshly ground black pepper
½ cup all-purpose flour
2 tablespoons olive oil
Spaetzle, page 127
Chopped fresh flat-leaf parsley,
   for serving

Remove the veal from the refrigerator and let it rest at room temperature for about 15 minutes.

In a medium saucepan, melt the butter over medium-low heat and cook the shallots for 2 to 3 minutes or until softened but not colored. Add the mushrooms, wine, and demi-glace and cook for 3 to 5 minutes or until soft.

Meanwhile, in a small bowl, stir together 2 tablespoons water and the cornstarch to make a slurry.

Add the heavy cream to the pan, raise the heat to medium-high, and cook for about 5 minutes until the cream reduces and thickens slightly. Reduce the heat to medium and stir in the cornstarch slurry to thicken the sauce further. Season to taste with salt and pepper. You will have about 1½ cups of very thick sauce. Cover the pan and keep warm over very low heat.

Put the flour in a shallow bowl and season with salt and pepper. Dip the veal in the flour to coat lightly on both sides. Shake the excess flour off the veal.

recipe continues on next page

In a large sauté pan, heat the oil over medium-high heat. Sauté the veal for 1 to 2 minutes, or until lightly browned, on both sides. You may have to sauté the veal in batches to avoid crowding the pan. If so, return all the meat to the pan when it is browned. Pour the mushroom sauce over the veal and simmer for about 2 minutes until the veal is cooked through. Do not let the sauce boil.

Serve the veal spooned over the hot spaetzle, garnished with parsley.

SPAETZLE

I grew up eating spaetzle, a staple in my homeland of Bavaria. They are perfect with sauced meats and fish because they sop up every last delicious drop. They are not difficult to make and are surprisingly light. **SERVES 4**

1⅓ cups all-purpose flour (about ½ pound)

3 large eggs

Pinch of freshly grated nutmeg

½ cup plus 1 tablespoon ice water

Salt and freshly ground white pepper

½ to 1 tablespoon sunflower or canola oil

1½ teaspoons unsalted butter

In the bowl of an electric mixer fitted with a dough hook, mix together the flour, eggs, nutmeg, cold water, and about ¼ teaspoon salt and ¼ teaspoon pepper. Mix on medium speed for 5 to 10 minutes or until the dough is still runny and thickened but not stiff. The dough will be sticky. This can be done by hand, with a wooden spoon, if you prefer.

Fill a large pot about two-thirds full with water. Season lightly with salt and bring to a boil over high heat. Meanwhile, fill a large bowl with ice and cold water and position near the stove.

Put the spaetzle dough on a damp cutting board or similar flat work surface. Break off a small portion of spaetzle and using a small, sharp knife, slice off pieces measuring about ¼ inch square and let them drop directly into the boiling water. (If you have a colander with large holes, you can push the spaetzle dough through it directly into the water.) Cook for 3 to 5 minutes, stirring occasionally, until the spaetzle bob to the surface and are glossy and firm. With a slotted spoon or handled strainer, lift the spaetzle from the water and plunge in the ice water.

Continue working in batches until all the spaetzle are cooked. Drain thoroughly and transfer the spaetzle to a lidded container large enough to hold them easily. Drizzle with oil so that the spaetzle do not stick together. (If not cooking right away, cover and refrigerate for up to 3 days.)

To cook, in a large, nonstick skillet, melt the butter over medium heat. Add the spaetzle and cook, stirring gently, for 6 to 8 minutes, or until golden brown and lightly crisp. Season with salt and pepper and serve.

VEAL SALTIMBOCCA

A classic Italian favorite, this veal dish is a cinch to make and a joy to eat. The flavor of the veal, enhanced by the prosciutto and fresh sage, is out of this world. Toothpicks hold the ingredients together during cooking, which takes only minutes. **SERVES 3 OR 4**

8 thin slices veal, each about 2 ounces, lightly pounded to an even thickness
Salt and freshly ground black pepper
16 fresh sage leaves

8 thin slices prosciutto
1 tablespoon olive oil
1 tablespoon unsalted butter

Remove the veal slices from the refrigerator and let them rest at room temperature for about 15 minutes.

Sprinkle both sides of the veal slices with salt and pepper.

Put 2 sage leaves on each slice and cover the leaves with a slice of prosciutto. Thread 2 toothpicks through the prosciutto and the sage to secure them to each slice of veal.

In a large sauté pan, heat the olive oil and butter over medium heat. When the butter melts, sauté the veal, prosciutto side down, for 2 to 3 minutes or until golden. Very carefully, turn the veal over and cook for 2 minutes longer or until cooked through.

Remove the toothpicks and serve the veal with the sage and prosciutto.

CALVES' LIVER
WITH APPLES, ONIONS, AND BACON

Fresh calves' liver is mild and tender and sometimes is referred to as veal liver. The thickness of the liver pieces should be uniform so that they cook evenly and quickly. Don't be tempted to salt them before cooking, because the salt can toughen them. The apple-onion-bacon mixture served with the liver is fantastic and even if you are not a liver lover, try this. You will be happy you did. **SERVES 4**

1 pound smoked bacon, cut into 1½-inch
    squares
3 large yellow onions, cut into ¼-inch-thick
    slices
Kosher salt and freshly ground black pepper
2 large Red Delicious apples, peeled, cored,
    and cut into ¾-inch-thick slices

Eight 4-ounce calves' livers, about ½ inch
    thick, sliced
All-purpose flour
2 tablespoons Clarified Butter, page 227
2 tablespoons canola oil

In a large sauté pan, fry the bacon over medium or medium-low heat until crisp. Remove it with a slotted spoon and drain on paper towels. Leave the bacon fat in the pan.

Add the onions and a pinch of salt and pepper to the pan and cook the onions for about 20 minutes or until golden brown. Add the apples and cook, stirring, for about 5 minutes or until the apples begin to soften.

Drain any excess fat from the pan and discard it. Return the bacon to the pan. Cover and keep warm over very low heat.

Lightly sprinkle the liver with pepper. Coat both sides with flour and shake off any excess.

In a large sauté pan, heat the butter and oil over medium-high heat and when nearly smoking, add the liver slices and cook for about 2 minutes on each side or until medium. You might have to do this in batches. Do not crowd the pan.

Season each liver slice with a pinch of salt and put 2 slices on each of 4 serving plates. Spoon the sauce over the liver and serve.

AUTUMN FEAST MENU

OYSTERS ROCKEFELLER, PAGE 45

MINNESOTA WILD RICE AND MUSHROOM SOUP, PAGE 79

ROASTED VEAL SHANKS, PAGE 132

SPAETZLE, PAGE 127

CRANBERRY-APPLE COBBLER, PAGE 212

———————

AMERICANO COCKTAIL, PAGE 20

ROASTED VEAL SHANKS

This is a winner—a dish I love to make because everyone is so admiring of it. I learned to cook meaty veal shanks this way from my sister-in-law, Angela, who lives in Bavaria, where this is a traditional holiday dish. Toward the end of cooking, you brush cream over the shanks, which glazes them very nicely and enhances the sauce. And the sauce is just delicious spooned over the meat as well as any accompanying spaetzle, egg noodles, or roasted potatoes. You will have to special order the veal shanks. **SERVES 6**

Two 3½- to 4-pound whole veal shanks, trimmed of gristle and excess fat

Vegetable oil cooking spray

1 cup coarsely chopped celery (about 2 large ribs)

1 cup coarsely chopped peeled carrots (about 2 large carrots)

1 cup coarsely chopped yellow onion (1 medium onion)

2 tablespoons chopped garlic

2 teaspoons herbes de Provence

1 tablespoon kosher salt

½ teaspoon freshly ground black pepper

8 tablespoons (1 stick) unsalted butter, melted

¾ cup heavy cream

¼ cup tomato paste

½ cup chicken broth, if needed

WINE RECOMMENDATION

A Bordeaux blend from Argentina is a nice accompaniment to this dish. The full-bodied red, with distinctive flavors of violets, black cherry, and black currant, works well with the richness of this dish. Cheval des Andes from Mendoza, Argentina, is a good choice.

Wines from Provence generally have a cedar, spice-box quality that pairs nicely with the herbes de Provence and garlic in this dish and have enough body to stand up to the bone-in veal shank. We suggest M. Chapoutier's, Coteaux d'Aix-en-Provence, and Coteaux d'Aix Terra Delecta.

Remove the shanks from the refrigerator and let them rest at room temperature for 30 to 60 minutes.

Preheat the oven to 350°F. Spray a large roasting pan with cooking oil spray.

Spread the celery, carrots, and onion evenly over the bottom of the pan.

In a small bowl, mix together the garlic, herbs, salt, and pepper and rub into the shanks on all sides. Be sure to use all of the mixture.

Lay the shanks on top of the vegetables. Drizzle with the melted butter and then roast, uncovered, for about 1½ hours, turning the shanks every 30 minutes to promote even browning. Add a little water to the pan if the vegetables appear dry and are browning too quickly.

After 1½ hours, baste the shanks with the heavy cream. Continue to cook for about 1 hour and 45 minutes (for a total of at least 3 hours and 15 minutes cooking time). Baste with the cream and the pan drippings every 20 minutes or so. The shanks are done when the meat is very tender when pierced with a fork. It should pull away from the bone.

Transfer the shanks to a serving platter and cover with aluminum foil to keep warm.

Spoon the pan drippings and vegetables into a saucepan. Stir in the tomato paste and bring to a boil over medium-high heat. Boil for 2 to 3 minutes or until well blended and very hot. Remove from the heat.

Using an immersion blender or handheld electric mixer, very carefully mix the sauce until smooth. Mix in up to ½ cup of chicken broth to thin the sauce.

Return the pan to the heat and return to the boil for about 1 minute. Strain the sauce through a mesh strainer, pushing on the solids with a spoon or spatula to release as much flavor as possible. (This may not be necessary if the vegetables are soft enough.) Discard the solids. You will have about 2 cups of sauce.

Cut chunks of meat from the shanks and slice the meat for serving. Pass the sauce on the side.

Weekend Brunch Menu

STEAK BENEDICT

We watch many of our guests leave the restaurant, leftovers packed up in their Morton's To-Go Bags. We hope some of them will wake up the next morning and decide to make this terrific steak Benedict. Everyone likes eggs Benedict as a brunch meal, but when the dish is made with steak in place of ham, it's an out-of-the-park home run! **SERVES 4**

8 large eggs

10 to 12 ounces leftover grilled steak, sliced (16 to 20 slices)

4 English muffins, split

½ cup Béarnaise Sauce, recipe follows

COCKTAIL RECOMMENDATION
Americano Cocktail; Morton's Champagne Cocktail

In 2 deep skillets filled about halfway with simmering water, poach the eggs, 4 eggs in each skillet, for 2 to 3 minutes or until the whites set. If you have a large enough skillet, you could poach all the eggs at one time. Take the skillet off the heat and set aside, with the eggs still in the hot water.

Working swiftly, heat a small nonstick sauté pan over medium heat and heat the slices of steak just until warm. You do not want to cook the steak further.

Meanwhile, toast the English muffins. Put 1 whole muffin on each of 4 serving plates. Top each muffin half with steak and an egg. Spoon béarnaise sauce over each egg and serve.

BÉARNAISE SAUCE

Rich, sinful hollandaise sauce turns into béarnaise with the addition of shallots, tarragon, white wine, and white-wine vinegar. Delicious! We particularly like it with eggs Benedict, and of course it's a natural with filet mignon and prime rib. **MAKES ABOUT 2 CUPS**

1 tablespoon white-wine vinegar

1 tablespoon dry white wine

1 teaspoon dried tarragon

½ teaspoon chopped shallot

2 cups Hollandaise Sauce, page 47

Salt

In a small nonreactive saucepan over medium heat, combine the vinegar, wine, tarragon, and shallot. Cook for 2 to 3 minutes, or until enough liquid evaporates so that it barely coats the bottom of the pan.

In the top of a double boiler set over simmering water, heat the hollandaise sauce, whisking to keep it from separating. Add the vinegar-shallot mixture and continue whisking until combined. Season to taste with a little salt.

MORTON'S MEATLOAF

We make our meatloaf with beef only, which should come as no surprise since we are a steakhouse. We've even tried it with waygu, which is kobe-style beef, but it's best with beef that is about 20 percent fat, because the fat provides succulent flavor and texture. Much of the fat cooks out of the beef and you can spoon it off. In our book, meatloaf is one of the best choices for a hearty homemade meal, and leftovers make particularly delicious sandwiches. **SERVES 6 TO 8**

1½ tablespoons unsalted butter

1½ cups finely diced yellow onion (1 large onion)

¾ cup finely diced celery (1 to 2 ribs)

1 tablespoon minced fresh thyme

1½ teaspoons minced garlic

1½ teaspoons paprika

⅓ cup tomato juice (we use Sacramento)

¾ cup chicken broth

2 large eggs, lightly beaten

1 cup finely crushed saltines (about 24 crackers), see Note

3 tablespoons chopped fresh flat-leaf parsley

1½ tablespoons soy sauce

1½ teaspoons Dijon mustard

1 teaspoon kosher salt

¾ teaspoon freshly ground black pepper

3 pounds ground sirloin

4½ ounces Monterey Jack cheese, shredded (1 heaping cup)

¼ cup Morton's Cocktail Sauce, recipe follows

WINE RECOMMENDATION
Petite Syrah from California has a full mouthfeel that holds up to the variety of spices used in this dish. It also has rich pepper, berry, and jammy notes that go shoulder to shoulder with the meatloaf. Try Spellbound Petite Sirah from Lodi.

BEER RECOMMENDATION
Full-bodied Belgian red-style ale has clove, citrus, and earth flavors that stand up to the strong spices in the meatloaf. We recommend Unibroue Maudite, from Chambly, Quebec, Canada.

Preheat the oven to 375°F.

In a sauté pan, melt the butter over medium heat. When it is melted, add the onion and celery and cook for 7 to 8 minutes or until tender and just beginning to brown.

Stir in the thyme, garlic, and paprika and cook, stirring, for about 1 minute just until fragrant. Reduce the heat to low, add the tomato juice, and cook for another 3 minutes, or until the sauce thickens a little. Remove from the heat and set aside to cool.

In a large mixing bowl, whisk together the chicken broth and eggs. Stir in the crackers, parsley, soy sauce, mustard, salt, and pepper. Spoon the tomato sauce into the bowl and stir until incorporated.

Add the beef and cheese to the bowl and mix gently but thoroughly with a wooden spoon or your hands. Transfer the meat mixture to a pan measuring approximately 12 by 8 inches and 3 inches deep and shape into a loaf that fits the pan and has about the same dimensions. A large round casserole dish will work well, too.

Bake in the middle of the oven for about 1 hour and 15 minutes or until an instant-read thermometer registers 140°F when inserted into the center of the loaf.

Spread the cocktail sauce over the top of the meatloaf and bake for about 15 minutes or until the sauce turns into a glaze. Remove from the oven, cover with aluminum foil, and set aside to rest for about 10 minutes.

Slice and serve the slices on a platter, or serve directly from the pan.

NOTE: To crush the saltines, put them in the bowl of a food processor fitted with the metal blade and pulse until evenly and finely crushed.

MORTON'S COCKTAIL SAUCE

As you might expect, we make a great cocktail sauce. Serve this with shrimp or crab meat as well as with the meatloaf. **MAKES ABOUT 2 CUPS**

½ cup bottled commercial
   horseradish
1¾ cups bottled chili sauce

¾ teaspoon Worcestershire sauce
¾ teaspoon fresh lemon juice
Salt and freshly ground white pepper

Line a fine-mesh sieve with cheesecloth. Strain the horseradish in the sieve for 2 to 3 minutes, or until reduced to ¼ cup. Squeeze the cheesecloth to extract all the liquid. Discard the liquid.

In a small mixing bowl, combine the strained horseradish, chili sauce, Worcestershire sauce, and lemon juice. Season to taste with salt and pepper. Whisk until completely blended. Serve immediately or transfer to a covered storage container and refrigerate for up to 7 days.

COLORADO BEEF BRISKET

After the initial cooking, which does not take long, the brisket cooks for several hours, leaving you free to go about other things and giving the kitchen ample time to fill with enticing aromas. We suggest you serve this with your favorite recipe for cornbread or corn muffins. For more heat, increase the number of chipotle chiles. **SERVES 4 TO 6**

3 pounds boneless beef brisket

½ teaspoon kosher salt

2 teaspoons olive oil

1 large yellow onion, coarsely chopped

1 tablespoon chili powder

One 12-ounce jar chili sauce

One 12-ounce can beer

1 canned chipotle chile, chopped (about 1½ teaspoons)

Chopped fresh cilantro, for serving

Remove the brisket from the refrigerator and let it rest at room temperature for 30 to 60 minutes.

Preheat the oven to 325°F.

Season the brisket on both sides with the salt.

In a large skillet, heat the oil over medium-high heat and when hot, brown the brisket for about 2 minutes on each side. Transfer to a roasting pan or deep baking dish large enough to hold the brisket and set aside.

Reduce the heat under the skillet to medium and cook the onion for 4 to 5 minutes, or until softened. Sprinkle the chili powder over the onion, stir to mix, and cook for about 1 minute longer.

Stir in the chili sauce, beer, and chipotle chile, bring to a boil, and then pour the mixture over the brisket. Cover tightly and bake for 2½ to 3 hours or until the meat is tender when pierced with a fork.

Transfer the brisket to a cutting board. There will be about 4 cups of sauce in the pan.

Cut the meat across the grain into ¼-inch-thick slices. Arrange on a serving platter and spoon some sauce over the brisket. Garnish with the cilantro and pass the remaining sauce on the side.

KLAUS'S
CORNED BEEF HASH

With the exception of the hash made from the recipe here, the best corned beef hash I have had was in old-style New York delis. I modeled my version on taste memories from the many hashes I sampled over the years. For the best results, I suggest including the end pieces from the corned beef. To make this truly authentic and truly delicious, don't leave out the poached eggs, which are a crowning glory. **SERVES 4**

1 tablespoon sunflower or canola oil

1 large onion, finely diced (1 ½ to 2 cups)

½ cup finely chopped celery

1 pound cooked corned beef, chopped into
    ¼-inch dice (about 4 cups)

½ cup beef broth

½ teaspoon Worcestershire sauce

½ teaspoon freshly ground black pepper

2 cups ¼-inch diced potatoes

Vegetable oil cooking spray

4 large eggs

Kosher salt

WINE RECOMMENDATION
Prosecco is an Italian sparkling wine with nice acidity and nuances of ripe citrus, white pepper, and pear. All this goes very well with the spices, Worcestershire sauce, and eggs. We like Maschio dei Cavalieri DOC from Valdobbiadene, Italy.

BEER RECOMMENDATION
The roasted malt and hops of Irish stout blend with the flavors of the spiced corned beef without overpowering the eggs. Our choice is Goose Island Dublin Stout from Goose Island Beer Company in Chicago.

In a large saucepan, heat the oil over medium heat and cook the onion and celery for about 3 minutes or until softened.

Add the corned beef to the pan and cook for about 2 minutes. Add the beef broth, Worcestershire sauce, and pepper. Cover and simmer for about 10 minutes, adjusting the heat up or down to maintain a simmer.

Add the potatoes and cook, uncovered, for about 10 minutes or until the excess moisture evaporates and the flavors blend. Remove from the heat and set aside to cool. Cover and refrigerate for at least 4 hours or overnight.

Spray a large, nonstick sauté pan with cooking spray and heat the pan over high heat. Add the hash mixture to the pan and cook for 8 to 10 minutes or until heated through and lightly browned.

Meanwhile, poach the eggs, or fry them sunny-side up.

Divide the hash among 4 plates. Slide the eggs on top of the hash and season with salt. Serve immediately.

MORTON'S CHOPPED STEAK

The secret to this simple recipe is to use ground sirloin. Try to buy it from a butcher who will grind it in front of you, or who assures you he grinds it at the store. The meat should be a nice, rosy red without any graying or brown spots. Ground sirloin has less fat than other cuts but should still be evenly mixed with creamy-looking, small particles of fat. Look for ground beef with an 80 to 20 ratio of lean meat to fat (although of late it's more common to find ground sirloin with a 90 to 10 ratio, which is okay, too). **SERVES 4**

½ tablespoon olive oil

½ cup finely diced yellow onion (1 small onion)

2 pounds ground sirloin

6 tablespoons tomato juice (we use Sacramento)

¼ cup finely chopped red bell pepper

¼ cup finely chopped green bell pepper

1 large egg, lightly beaten

½ tablespoon kosher salt

½ teaspoon freshly ground black pepper

Store-bought thick chili sauce, for serving

WINE RECOMMENDATION
The jammy fruit of primitivo, the mother of the Zinfandel grape, marries nicely with the complex flavors of the chopped steak. Try A-Mano Zinfandel from Apulia (Puglia), Italy.

BEER RECOMMENDATION
Sweet malt with toasty grain flavors matches well with the chili sauce, peppers, and tomato juice while having enough body to work well with the sirloin. We like Bell's Amber Ale, from Kalamazoo, Michigan.

Preheat the broiler and position a rack 4 inches from the heating element.

In a small sauté pan, heat the olive oil over medium-low heat and sauté the onion for 3 to 5 minutes or until tender and lightly browned. Set aside to cool slightly.

In a large bowl, use your hands to gently mix the ground beef with the tomato juice, both bell peppers, egg, salt, black pepper, and cooled onions.

Shape into 4 oval patties, each about 1 inch thick.

Put the patties on a broiler pan and broil for about 7 minutes. Turn with a spatula and broil the other side for 6 to 8 minutes for medium-rare or until the desired degree of doneness.

Serve with the chili sauce.

MORTON'S SHORT RIBS

Short ribs are very popular these days, which I think makes a lot of sense. They are true comfort food with deep beef flavor that satisfies as only a long-cooked braise can. Like most braises, this is best made a day ahead of serving and then reheated. The flavors will have had time to be absorbed by the meat and also to have infused the sauce during this time. The potatoes and mushrooms will mingle gorgeously with the ribs and sauce for an unforgettable meal. **SERVES 6**

SHORT RIBS

6 pounds bone-in beef short ribs

6 ounces chopped bacon (6 to 8 slices)

1 tablespoon salt

½ tablespoon freshly ground black pepper

½ cup all-purpose flour

1 tablespoon olive oil

1 large yellow onion, coarsely chopped
   (about 2 cups)

1 carrot, peeled and diced

2 ribs celery, diced

One 750-ml bottle full-bodied dry red wine

3 cloves garlic, chopped

1½ tablespoons tomato paste

1 tablespoon store-bought beef or veal
   demi-glace, see Note, page 117, or beef
   broth

1 sprig of fresh rosemary

One 2-ounce chunk of Parmesan cheese

VEGETABLES

5 very small red potatoes, halved (about
   6 ounces)

1 rib celery, cut in 1½-inch pieces

1 tablespoon unsalted butter

2 ounces white mushrooms, sliced (about 1 cup)

2 to 3 sprigs of fresh rosemary, for serving

2 tablespoons chopped fresh flat-leaf parsley,
   for serving

WINE RECOMMENDATION

The rustic edge of the Tempranillo grape is a good bet for this rustic dish. We suggest Vega Sicilia Unico from Ribera del Duero, Spain. With several years of oak aging, this wine plays well off of the bacon and beef in this dish. The plum, blackberry, and jammy nature of Malbec wine match the richness of the short ribs, too. Our choice is Catena Zapata Malbec from Mendoza, Argentina.

Remove the ribs from the refrigerator and let them rest at room temperature for 30 to 60 minutes.

Preheat the oven to 400°F.

In a large nonreactive sauté pan, cook the bacon over medium-low heat for 3 to 5 minutes or until cooked but not crisp. Using a slotted spoon, remove the bacon from the pan and drain on paper towels. Do not wipe the pan clean.

In a small dish, mix together the salt and pepper. Rub it on all sides of the ribs.

Spread the flour in a shallow dish and dip the ribs in the flour to coat. Shake off the excess.

In the pan with the bacon fat, brown the ribs on all sides over medium heat; this will take 15 to 20 minutes. (You will have to do this in batches so as not to crowd the pan.) Use tongs to hold the ribs in the pan if need be so that each side browns nicely in the fat. Transfer the ribs to a roasting pan large enough to hold them in a single layer. Pour the grease out of the sauté pan and discard.

Add the olive oil to the sauté pan, reduce the heat to medium-low, and sauté the onion, carrot, and celery for 6 to 8 minutes or until softened. Stir in the wine, garlic, tomato paste, and demi-glace, bring to a simmer, and cook for about 5 minutes or until blended. Stir in the rosemary sprig, bacon and Parmesan chunk. Pour this sauce over the ribs.

Cover the roasting pan and roast the ribs for 1 hour. Reduce the oven temperature to 350°F and continue roasting for about 30 minutes, or until the meat is tender and falls off the bone.

Meanwhile, in a medium pot filled halfway with boiling salted water, cook the potatoes for 6 to 8 minutes over medium-high heat, or until nearly tender when pierced with the tip of a small, sharp knife but not completely cooked through. Remove with a slotted spoon and set aside. Add the celery and cook for 2 to 3 minutes or until tender and bright green. Drain well.

In a large sauté pan, melt the butter over medium heat and when bubbling, add the mushrooms, potatoes, and celery and cook for 8 to 10 minutes or until the potatoes are cooked through and the mushrooms soften and release their moisture. Set aside, covered, to keep warm.

Remove ribs from the pan and set aside, covered to keep warm. With an immersion blender or in a food processor fitted with the metal blade and working in batches, purée the sauce from the roasting pan. You will have about 3 ½ cups of textured sauce.

Return the ribs to the roasting pan or put them in a large skillet. Pour the puréed sauce over the ribs. Set over medium-high heat and bring to a simmer. Cook for about 10 minutes or until heated through.

Arrange the ribs and sauce on a large serving platter and spoon the potato and mushroom mixture around the ribs. Garnish with the fresh rosemary and chopped parsley.

HERB-CRUSTED LAMB LOIN

I am particularly fond of loin of lamb, which is easy to cook, easy to slice, and, naturally, extremely easy to eat. Not surprisingly it is delectably tender. This is a wonderful party dish and a little different from the expected fare. You can make this with two eight-bone racks of lamb, too. **SERVES 6**

2 pieces boneless lamb loin (each 18 to 19 ounces), trimmed of silver skin

Kosher salt and freshly ground black pepper

8 tablespoons (1 stick) unsalted butter, softened

3 tablespoons dry bread crumbs

2 tablespoons chopped fresh rosemary

2 tablespoons chopped fresh basil

2 tablespoons chopped fresh flat-leaf parsley

1 tablespoon Dijon mustard

1 teaspoon chopped garlic

¼ teaspoon Worcestershire sauce

2 tablespoons olive oil

WINE RECOMMENDATION

Hungarian red wine can be complex and meaty and so is a glorious accompaniment to the lamb loin. The blend of up to eight different grapes offers earthy aromas and flavors that are every bit as splendid as that of the lamb and herbs but do not clash with the spiciness of the mustard or Worcestershire sauce. We recommend Bull's Blood from Eger, Hungary.

The red cherry and raspberry notes of Carmenere wine from Chile will play nicely with the rosemary, basil, and parsley. The silky texture and medium tannins will not overpower the balance of this dish. Try LaPlaya from Maipo Valley in Chile.

Remove the lamb chops from the refrigerator and let them rest at room temperature for 30 to 60 minutes.

Preheat the oven to 450°F.

Season the lamb loins with salt and pepper.

In a small bowl, mix together the butter, bread crumbs, rosemary, basil, parsley, mustard, garlic, and Worcestershire sauce to form a paste. Season to taste with salt and pepper (you will need at least ¼ teaspoon of each).

In a large sauté pan, heat the olive oil over high heat. Sear the loins on all sides for about 1½ minutes per side. Remove the lamb from the heat and let it cool until easy to handle.

Spread the seasoned butter over the top of the loins and transfer to a roasting pan. Roast for 11 to 12 minutes for medium rare.

Remove the lamb from the oven and turn on the broiler. Broil the meat for about 1 minute to crisp up the coating. Let the lamb rest for about 5 minutes before serving.

RACK OF LAMB WELLINGTON

Everyone has heard of beef Wellington, but Wellington made with lamb is something of a novelty—and yet totally delicious. The breading keeps the meat moist and juicy but the crust is not in the least soggy. Preparing this sounds more difficult than it is. Once you start, the method for wrapping the racks with the puff pastry and phyllo dough combo will make perfect sense. **SERVES 8**

BLACKBERRY JUS

1 tablespoon vegetable oil

½ cup finely chopped celery

½ cup finely chopped carrot

½ cup finely chopped onion

4 ounces lamb bones (if available) or about
    1 cup lamb scraps from racks of lamb,
    see Note

½ cup dry red wine

1 tablespoon tomato paste

1 teaspoon whole black peppercorns

1 small bay leaf

2 fresh sage leaves, torn

⅓ cup fresh blackberries

½ teaspoon sugar

Kosher salt

FILLING

2 tablespoons unsalted butter

¼ cup minced shallots

3½ ounces medium white mushrooms, thinly
    sliced (about 3 cups)

3½ ounces shiitake mushrooms, stemmed and
    thinly sliced (about 3 cups)

½ cup heavy cream

5 tablespoons pine nuts, toasted

2 large eggs

2 sheets puff pastry, defrosted, see Note

2 sheets phyllo dough, see Note

Four 8-bone racks of lamb (each 16 to 18 ounces),
    excess fat trimmed, frenched, see Note

WINE RECOMMENDATION
The lush black fruit and pepper flavors of California Zinfandel match this dish, flavor for flavor. Try Kunde Estate, Sonoma, California.

The combination of Cabernet and Grenache that make up Priorat wines creates big statements with mineral, earth, and blackberry notes. When paired with this dish, they enhance the subtle nuances of mushrooms, shallots, and sage.

To make the jus: In a medium saucepan, heat the oil over high heat and when hot, cook the celery, carrot, onion, and lamb bones for 3 to 4 minutes or until the vegetables soften and the bones brown.

Stir in the wine and scrape the bottom of the pan with a wooden spoon to release any browned bits. Add the tomato paste, peppercorns, and bay leaf and cook for 1 to 2 minutes or until well incorporated. Add 3 cups water and the sage,

recipe continues on page 148

bring to a boil, and partially cover the pan. Reduce the heat and simmer for about 40 minutes or until there is about ⅔ cup of sauce in the pan. Adjust the heat up or down to maintain the simmer.

Strain the sauce through a fine-mesh sieve into a bowl. Discard the solids. Spoon the fat from the surface of the sauce and discard the fat.

Return the sauce to the saucepan and add the blackberries. Warm over medium heat for 8 to 10 minutes or just until the berries begin to soften. Strain the sauce through a fine-mesh sieve, pressing on the berries to extract the seeds. Discard the solids. Return the jus to the saucepan and bring to a simmer. Cook for 3 to 5 minutes or until slightly thickened.

Stir the sugar into the sauce until dissolved. Season to taste with salt. You should have a scant ½ cup of jus at this point. Cover and set aside to keep warm.

To make the filling: In a medium sauté pan, melt the butter over medium heat, add the shallots, and cook for about 3 minutes or until softened. Add the mushrooms, cover the pan, and cook for about 5 minutes or until tender and the mushrooms release their liquid. Stir in the cream and bring to a simmer. Simmer for about 4 minutes or until the cream thickens and most of the moisture evaporates. Set aside to cool.

In the bowl of a food processor fitted with the metal blade, process the filling until nearly smooth but some small chunks of mushroom remain. Stir in the pine nuts and season to taste with salt and pepper.

Whisk the eggs with ¼ cup water to make an egg wash.

On a lightly floured surface, roll the puff pastry just until slightly larger and thinner than it already is. Cut each piece of puff pastry in half crosswise and set aside, covered with a well-wrung, damp kitchen towel. Put the phyllo dough under the same or a similar kitchen towel.

Working with 1 piece of puff pastry at a time, lightly brush it on 1 side with the egg wash and then prick several times with a fork. Cover the pastry with half of a sheet of phyllo and pat the phyllo into the pastry so that it adheres. Put 1 rack of lamb on one end of the dough so that 1 inch of the frenched bones extends over the edge of the dough and the fat-covered side is face-up.

Spread a quarter of the mushroom filling on the top of the rack. Wrap the rack tightly in the dough by folding the dough in half and pressing the sides together. The dough will cover the meat portion of the rack, not the exposed bones. Using a small, sharp knife, cut the dough between the bones and press and fit to seal. Put the package on a parchment-paper-lined baking pan and brush the dough with egg wash. Repeat with the remaining 3 racks. If you make these ahead of time, refrigerate until ready to cook or for up to 6 hours. Let the packages come to room temperature before baking. This takes about 1 hour.

Preheat the oven to 450°F.

Bake the dough-wrapped racks of lamb for 15 to 16 minutes. Reduce the oven temperature to 375°F and continue baking for 10 to 12 minutes longer or until the pastry is puffed and golden. Remove from the oven and let the meat rest for 5 to 10 minutes and before slicing between the bones. (An electric knife is great for this.) Reheat the jus over very low heat and serve on the side.

NOTE: To french the bones of the racks, trim the excess fat and meat from the tops of the bones, about 3 or 4 inches down the bone. Reserve the scraps from this for the jus. You can ask the butcher to french the racks for you, but remember to ask for the scraps, which should measure about 1 cup.

Pepperidge Farm makes very good frozen puff pastry. The sheets come two to a box and so you will only need a single box for this recipe. Phyllo dough, also called filo, is sold by weight, and a one-pound box generally yields 20 to 24 thin sheets, each measuring approximately 12 by 18 inches. Use what you need and then refreeze the rest for another recipe.

WINTER DINNER PARTY MENU

TUNA TARTARE, PAGE 41

NEW YORK SIRLOIN STRIP ROAST WITH THREE-PEPPERCORN SAUCE, PAGE 115

BAKED ONIONS WITH GRUYÈRE, PAGE 190

SAUTÉED GARLIC GREEN BEANS, PAGE 191

CRANBERRY-APPLE COBBLER, PAGE 212

SAZERAC, PAGE 19

POMEGRANATE-SAKE COCKTAIL, PAGE 20

LAMB CHOPS PICCATA

These lamb chops cook in minutes and taste sensational. Once you flatten the chops, there is nothing more to it—and what a tasty departure from veal or chicken piccata! **SERVES 2**

Twelve 2-ounce petite lamb rib chops,
    frenched, see Note
Kosher salt and freshly ground black pepper
All-purpose flour
2 large eggs, lightly beaten

6 tablespoons (¾ stick) unsalted butter or
    Clarified Butter, page 227
¼ cup drained capers, rinsed and drained again
2 tablespoons fresh lemon juice
Chopped fresh flat-leaf parsley, for serving

WINE RECOMMENDATION
The blend of Carignan, Grenache, and Syrah grapes gives Languedoc red wines cherry, plum, and blackberry notes and a peppery finish that balance well with the richness of the lamb and the acidity of the capers and lemon juice. We suggest Château Véronique from Languedoc, France.

Remove the chops from the refrigerator and let them rest at room temperature for 30 to 60 minutes.

Put the chops between sheets of wax paper or plastic wrap and using a meat mallet, pound the eye of the chop (the meat only; not the bone) until as thin as possible without tearing it. This is tricky to do. Don't worry if you can't pound it too thin. Remove the paper and lightly season the chops with salt and pepper on both sides.

Put the flour in a shallow dish and the eggs in another. Dip the seasoned lamb chops into the flour, shaking off any excess, and then into the eggs, letting the excess drip off.

In a large sauté pan, heat 2 tablespoons of the butter over medium heat and when it bubbles, cook half of the chops for about 30 seconds. Do not crowd the pan. Turn the chops over, add half the capers and half the lemon juice, and cook for about 30 seconds longer. Remove the chops to a warm plate and cover to keep warm.

Repeat with 2 tablespoons of butter and the remaining chops, capers, and lemon juice. Lift the chops from the pan and set aside, covered, to keep warm.

Add the remaining 2 tablespoons butter to the pan and cook the sauce for about 30 seconds or until lightly browned.

Put 6 chops on each plate and pour the sauce over them. Garnish each plate with parsley and serve.

NOTE: Frenched chops are those with the meat scraped from the bone so that only the eye, or round part, of the meat remains.

STUFFED PORK CHOPS

Years ago, when I cooked at a restaurant in Switzerland, I made a similar dish and was impressed with the flavor of the cheese and the mortadella sausage with the pork. It's not difficult to make a pocket in the side of a pork chop, but if you are nervous about it, ask the butcher for help. **SERVES 2**

Two 8-ounce center-cut pork chops

2 thin slices mortadella sausage

4 thin slices provolone cheese

2 fresh sage leaves

Kosher salt and freshly ground black pepper

¼ cup all-purpose flour

1 large egg, slightly beaten

1½ cups Morton's Bread Crumbs, page 153

5 tablespoons extra-virgin olive oil

2 tablespoons unsalted butter

WINE RECOMMENDATION
The nero d'avola grape makes a light to medium bodied wine with notes of mint, violets, and chocolate that brings forth the sage and the subtle notes of the mortadella. We suggest "Saia," Feudo Maccari, Sicily.

The cherry and herb characteristics of American grenache work well with the sage, pistachio, and garlic-laced mortadella. It has a medium body strong enough to stand together with the pork and provolone. Try Bonny Doon, "Le Cigar Volant," Santa Cruz, California.

Remove the chops from the refrigerator and let them rest at room temperature for 30 to 60 minutes.

Preheat the oven to 400°F.

On the thickest side of each chop, cut a deep pocket in the meat as far as the bone. Wiggle the knife in the meat to open the pocket but do not cut all the way through.

Fold 1 slice of mortadella into a rectangle slightly smaller than the pocket. Put the folded mortadella in the center of a slice of provolone and fold the provolone over the mortadella to encase it. Push the little package into the pocket of a chop and then insert a sage leaf. Repeat with the other pork chop. Secure the pockets' opening with a small metal or wooden skewer and press on the meat to flatten it over and below the pocket.

Season the chops with salt and pepper. Lightly dust them on both sides with flour and shake off the excess.

Put the egg in a shallow bowl and the bread crumbs in another. Dip the floured chops in the egg and then in the bread crumbs to coat. Gently press the crumbs into the meat on all sides.

In an ovenproof, medium sauté pan, heat the oil and butter over medium-high heat until

recipe continues on page 153

the oil is hot and the butter melted. Cook the chops for about 2 minutes on each side or until golden brown. Transfer to the oven and bake for 15 to 18 minutes or until cooked through and an instant-read thermometer inserted in the thickest part of the chops registers 155°F. Let the chops rest for 5 to 10 minutes and serve.

MORTON'S BREAD CRUMBS

It's very easy to make fresh bread into crumbs in the food processor or blender. While this recipe doesn't call for stale bread, you can use it here if you have some. I suggest you pat the garlic and shallot dry before adding them to the crumbs for more efficient mixing. We use these to bread shrimp, cod, crab cakes, and chicken; you'll use them for all sorts of recipes that call for bread crumbs.

MAKES ABOUT 2 CUPS

8 ounces firm white bread
   (4 to 5 standard-size slices)
5 teaspoons minced garlic
2 teaspoons minced shallot

2 teaspoons chopped fresh flat- or
   curly-leaf parsley
Salt and freshly ground black pepper

Slice the crusts from the bread and then cut the bread into large chunks. Discard the crusts or reserve them for another use.

In the bowl of a food processor fitted with the metal blade, grind the bread to fine crumbs. Transfer the crumbs to a mixing bowl.

Pat the garlic and shallot dry with a paper towel. Add to the bread crumbs and toss to mix. Add the parsley, toss, and season to taste with salt and pepper. Mix well. Use right away or store the bread crumbs in a tightly covered container in the refrigerator for up to 24 hours.

TUSCAN PORK CHOPS

Thick, lightly breaded pork chops are topped with a lovely pepper-and-tomato ragout subtly flavored with garlic and basil. This combination makes a light, fresh-tasting dish—even in the dead of winter. **SERVES 4**

SWEET PEPPER RAGOUT

12 ounces plum tomatoes (4 to 5 tomatoes)

3 tablespoons extra-virgin olive oil

½ cup thinly sliced red bell pepper

½ cup thinly sliced green bell pepper

¼ cup thinly sliced red onion

2 teaspoons sliced garlic

2 teaspoons thinly slivered fresh basil leaves

Salt and freshly ground black pepper

PORK CHOPS

Four 8-ounce bone-in loin pork chops, about 1 inch thick

Salt and freshly ground black pepper

½ cup all-purpose flour

2 large eggs

1½ cups Tuscan Bread Crumbs, page 226

2 tablespoons olive oil

WINE RECOMMENDATION
A full-bodied Chianti from Italy, with essences of violets, cherries, plums, and herbs, brings out the best in this dish. Our choice is Ruffino Chianti Riserva Ducale Oro from Tuscany.

BEER RECOMMENDATION
Italian pilsner has light citrus and hoppy notes that pair well with the acidity of the sweet pepper ragout without overpowering the pork. We recommend Nastro Azzurro from Rome.

To make the ragout: Halve the tomatoes and gently squeeze out the seeds. Quarter them lengthwise and slice across the quarters to make thin pieces, about ⅜ inch wide.

In a large sauté pan, heat the olive oil over medium heat. When hot, add both types of bell pepper, the onion, garlic, and tomatoes and cook for about 4 minutes, or until the tomatoes are very soft and the peppers and onion are cooked but still al dente.

Add the basil and season to taste with salt and pepper. Cook for about 1 minute or until the flavors blend. Set aside and keep warm.

To prepare the pork chops: Preheat the oven to 400°F. Season the pork chops with salt and pepper and dust each with flour.

Whisk the eggs and 2 tablespoons of water together in a shallow bowl and put the bread crumbs in another bowl.

Dip the chops in the egg wash to coat on both sides and then dip into the bread crumbs so that they are completely coated.

In a 10-inch sauté pan, heat the oil over medium heat. When hot, cook the chops for about 2 minutes on each side, or until they are golden brown. Transfer the chops to a shallow baking pan.

Bake the chops for 8 to 9 minutes. Turn and bake for 8 to 9 minutes longer or until cooked through. An instant-read thermometer inserted into the center of the meat will register 150°F.

Meanwhile warm up the sweet pepper ragout. Divide equally among 4 serving plates. Lay the chops partially on the ragout and serve immediately.

OLD-FASHIONED ROASTED PORK LOIN

This pork roast is so simple and straightforward: It's the quintessential Sunday dinner roast that tastes delicious with mashed or roasted potatoes. Like most roasts, it's easy to cook and slices beautifully. Be sure to let it rest for about 10 minutes before carving to give the interior juices time to redistribute throughout the meat. **SERVES 6**

1 tablespoon garlic salt (or 1 tablespoon kosher salt mixed with 1 crushed clove garlic)

1 tablespoon freshly ground black pepper

1 tablespoon herbes de Provence

½ tablespoon sweet paprika

One 4½-pound center-cut pork loin with bone

1 large carrot, cut into chunks

1 large rib celery, cut into chunks

1 medium onion, cut into chunks

2 bay leaves

½ cup dry white wine

1 cup reconstituted store-bought veal demi-glace, see Note, page 117

WINE RECOMMENDATION
French Viogniers from the northern Rhône region of France have a rich "fattiness" to them that gives them the ability to match well with a fuller meat, such as a bone-in pork roast. The almond, peach, and apricot notes of the grape lend themselves well to the rustic herbes de Provence that flavor this dish. Our choice is Château-Grillet.

French Pinot Noir, with its earthy flavors, medium body, and medium tannin, creates a mouth-feel that is wonderful with the pork. We like Griotte Chambertin from Burgundy, France.

In a small bowl, stir together the garlic salt, pepper, herbes de Provence, and paprika and rub the mixture into the pork. Cover the meat and refrigerate for at least 3 hours or up to 12 hours.

Preheat the oven to 350°F.

Remove the pork from the refrigerator and let it sit at room temperature for about 15 minutes.

Put the pork in a flame-proof roasting pan and roast uncovered for about 1 hour.

Scatter the carrot, celery, onion, and bay leaves around the meat and roast for about 15 minutes longer.

Remove the roasting pan from the oven and add 1 cup water to it. Using a wooden spoon, scrape the browned bits from the bottom of the pan. Return the pan to the oven and roast for about 20 minutes longer or until the internal temperature of the pork reaches 140°F. The pork is not completely cooked at this point. Do not turn off the oven.

Remove the roast from the pan, transfer to a cutting board, and cover it with foil to keep it warm. Put the roasting pan on a stovetop burner over high heat. Scrape the browned bits from the bottom of the pan. Add the wine, bring to a boil, and cook for about 5 minutes. Add the demi-glace and cook for 1 to 2 minutes longer or until the sauce blends.

Strain the sauce through a sieve, pushing down on the vegetables to extract as much flavor as possible. Discard the vegetables and keep the sauce warm. You will have about 2 cups of sauce.

Return the pork to the roasting pan and roast for 20 minutes longer. Transfer the pork to a cutting board and let it rest for about 10 minutes.

Slice the pork into thin pieces. Arrange them on a platter, spoon the sauce over the meat, and serve. Pass the remaining sauce on the side.

↩ CELEBRITY CLIP ↩

TORONTO HAS QUICKLY become Hollywood of the North, with many of the biggest-name entertainers now regularly attending its annual film festival in September. Morton's in Toronto has certainly seen its share of top TV and movie stars in recent years. After coming in a few months earlier while on tour, Justin Timberlake arrived recently with Jessica Biel for the filet and Morton's Legendary Hot Chocolate Cake. Soon after, we welcomed Ontario native Rachel McAdams, who hosted a surprise birthday party for her parents. On one night during the film festival, we hosted Jude Law and friends, as well as Sean Penn, Liv Tyler, and Sienna Miller dining together. To cap it off the following night, Brad Pitt and Angelina Jolie celebrated the premier of Brad's movie *The Assassination of Jesse James by the Coward Robert Ford,* with Casey Affleck (who played Robert Ford) and Don Cheadle. Brad and Angie had the filet. Our Toronto Morton's has never had so many paparazzi camped out in front of the restaurant as were there that evening. YouTube even ran the top-rated video of Brad and Angelina at Morton's on its website! ↩

BARBECUED BABY BACK RIBS

Our executive chef, Chris Rook, developed the sauce for these baby backs, which is both Asian-inspired and spiked with bourbon. Perhaps not a traditional take on a barbecue sauce, but awfully good. Once these are cooked, the meat is tender and tasty and just about impossible to resist. If you want extra sauce to pass alongside the ribs, double the sauce and set half aside to heat just before serving. When we make these, the racks feed four or five of us, but we really like ribs. You might be able to get a few more servings. **SERVES 4 TO 6**

RIBS

1½ teaspoons dry English mustard

1½ teaspoons sweet paprika

1½ teaspoons salt

1½ teaspoons freshly ground black pepper

About 8½ pounds baby back pork ribs
   (3 to 4 racks)

¾ cup pineapple juice (6 ounces)

Vegetable oil cooking spray

SAUCE

½ cup ketchup

3 tablespoons bourbon

2 tablespoons hoisin garlic sauce

2 tablespoons plum sauce

2 tablespoons balsamic vinegar

2 tablespoons honey

2 tablespoons Dijon mustard

1 teaspoon Worcestershire sauce

½ teaspoon hot red pepper paste

½ teaspoon freshly ground black pepper

WINE RECOMMENDATION
The bright fruit flavors of a dry Lambrusco are the perfect pairing for barbecue. Try Riunite Vivante sparkling Lambrusco from Italy.

BEER RECOMMENDATION
A light-style porter pairs nicely with the barbecued pork recipe. The toffee and coffee notes bring out the complex flavors of the sauce while the bitter, malty side of the beer provides a fresh, clean finish. We like Road Dog Porter from the Flying Dog Brewery in Maryland.

To cook the ribs: Preheat the oven to 350°F.

In a small bowl, stir together the mustard, paprika, salt, and pepper. Rub the mixture over both sides of the racks of ribs and put the racks in a large roasting pan. They can overlap each other in the pan. Pour the pineapple juice over the ribs, cover tightly with aluminum foil, and bake for about 1¼ hours or until the ribs are cooked through but not so tender the meat begins to pull away from the bones. Do not overcook the ribs at this point or they will fall apart on the grill.

To prepare a charcoal or gas grill, lightly spray the grill

recipe continues on next page

rack with cooking spray before lighting. The coals should be medium for the charcoal grill. The burners should be on medium for the gas grill.

To make the sauce: In a mixing bowl, whisk together the ketchup, bourbon, hoisin sauce, plum sauce, vinegar, honey, mustard, Worcestershire, red pepper paste, and black pepper. You will have about 1⅓ cups of sauce. (The sauce can be prepared a day ahead, covered, and refrigerated until needed.)

Lift the ribs from the roasting pan and lay on a work surface. Discard the cooking juices. Brush the ribs on both sides with the sauce; you will use about 2 tablespoons of sauce per side. Grill the racks for 10 to 15 minutes total, turning once. The sauce will begin to caramelize and brown, at which point the racks should be turned.

Cut the ribs between the bones and serve.

OLD-FASHIONED ROASTED CHICKEN

Just about everyone can roast a chicken, but we like to plan ahead and let ours marinate for a day or so before cooking. We rub the chickens with olive oil, butter, and herbs and other flavorings, wrap them tightly in plastic wrap, and refrigerate. The roasted birds are gloriously juicy with exceedingly crispy skin. While this dish is good made with any chicken, I recommend free-range, Amish-style, or organic birds. These chickens simply taste better than others. **SERVES 6 TO 8**

Two 3½- to 4-pound chickens, preferably
    Amish or free-range

2 tablespoons olive oil

2 tablespoons unsalted butter, softened

1 tablespoon Worcestershire sauce

Juice of 1 lemon

2 teaspoons crushed dried oregano

2 teaspoons salt-free lemon pepper

1 teaspoon sweet Hungarian paprika

1 teaspoon salt

½ cup chicken broth or water

WINE RECOMMENDATION

The Alto Adige region of Italy is a great spot to grow the Germanic grape, Müller Thurgau. The spicy notes and flavors of dried apricots and herbs are a great match for the oregano, Worcestershire sauce, and chicken. We like Cantina Santa Maddalena from Alto Adige, Italy.

This dish pairs well with the earthy style, light body, and light tannins of Pinot Noir from Oregon. The light scents of earth, strawberries, and rose petal will match well with the paprika and the oregano. Try Fiddlehead Cellar's Pinot Noirs from the Willamette Valley in Oregon.

Rinse the chickens inside and outside with cold water and pat dry. Let them rest at room temperature for 30 to 60 minutes.

In a small bowl, stir together the olive oil, butter, Worcestershire sauce, and lemon juice.

In another small bowl, mix together the oregano, lemon pepper, paprika, and salt.

Brush the chickens with the butter mixture and then season with the herbs. Put the chickens in a glass or similar container, cover with plastic wrap or a lid, and refrigerate for at least 8 and up to 24 hours.

Preheat the oven to 375°F.

Remove the chickens from the refrigerator and let them sit on the counter for about 30 minutes or until they reach room temperature.

Put the chickens in a roasting pan and using your fingers, make sure the butter is evenly spread over the chickens. Roast in the center of the oven for about 1 hour and 20 minutes,

recipe continues on page 163

basting once or twice with the pan drippings. If the chickens brown too quickly, tent them loosely with aluminum foil.

Raise the oven temperature to 400°F and cook the chickens for an additional 12 to 15 minutes, or until an instant-read thermometer registers 175°F when inserted in the breast meat.

Transfer the chickens to a cutting board and let them rest for about 10 minutes.

Meanwhile, add the broth to the roasting pan and bring to a boil over 1 or 2 burners set on medium-high heat. Stir for 1 to 2 minutes, scraping up any browned bits stuck on the bottom of the pan. Season to taste with salt and pepper, if necessary.

Cut each chicken into 8 serving pieces and serve on a large platter, with the pan drippings spooned over them.

ᔥ CELEBRITY CLIP ᔥ

MORTON'S THE STEAKHOUSE is a favorite dining destination for celebrities, and word travels fast: We find that the cast, crew, and producers of certain television shows often dine with us. For instance, Kevin Connolly, one of the stars of the HBO series *Entourage,* and the show's supervising producer, Brian Burns, are regulars at our Beverly Hill's Morton's. Other cast and crew members frequently join them, including Jerry Ferrara who plays Turtle on the award-winning show. When ABC's *Desperate Housewives* first hit the scene, we quickly saw the actors of that show and their guests dining with us around the country. William H. Macy threw a surprise party for his wife, Felicity Huffman, at Morton's, which included bringing in a microphone and band so that Mr. Macy could serenade his wife. Teri Hatcher hosted a surprise seventieth birthday party for her mother on a Sunday evening, after which some of her guests went into the bar to watch the evening's episode of the show. Eva Longoria and her just-as-famous husband, Tony Parker, star player of the San Antonio Spurs, dine often with us in San Antonio, Texas, and elsewhere throughout the country. Even Marcia Cross, who plays the inimitable Bree Hodge on the show, has dined with us more than a few times. But it leaves us wondering, where have you been, Nicolette Sheridan? We have a table waiting for you! ᔥ

STUFFED CHICKEN BREASTS

The cheese-and-spinach filling for these chicken breasts is lovely, and once the breasts are stuffed, they stay moist and tender during cooking. We bone the meat and keep the skin on the breasts, but since it's not always easy to find skin-on, boned breasts, you might have to ask the butcher to do this for you. Sliced for serving, the chicken is very pretty.

SERVES 4

3 tablespoons olive oil, or more if needed

4 cloves garlic, thinly sliced

4 ounces fresh baby spinach (approximately 5½ cups)

Salt and freshly ground black pepper

1 large plum tomato, seeded and diced

5 teaspoons chopped fresh basil leaves or thyme, plus more for serving

9 ounces fresh goat cheese, softened

4 large whole, boneless chicken breasts, skin on, see Note

2 tablespoons minced shallots

1 cup dry white wine

2 cups heavy cream

¼ teaspoon chicken base, see Note, page 81

WINE RECOMMENDATION
Spanish rosés are crisp and fruity and a good choice for light meats with rich fillings. Try Marques de Caceres Rosé from Rioja, Spain.

Vouvrays have a slight sweetness to them that works well with the richness of the cheese and the acidity of the spinach. The wines have pear and anise notes that carry the basil and the shallots along, despite the richness of the cheese, and create a perfect balance of flavors. Our choice is Champalou Vouvray from the Loire Valley in France.

Preheat the oven to 350°F.

In a sauté pan, heat 1 tablespoon of the olive oil over medium-high heat and when hot, add 3 cloves of the garlic and cook for about 1 minute or until light golden brown. Add the spinach to the pan, season with a pinch each of salt and pepper, and cook for 1 to 2 minutes, or until the spinach wilts.

Stir in the tomato and cook for about 30 seconds, or just until the tomato and spinach are well mixed. Stir in 4 teaspoons of the chopped basil and, as soon as the herbs are well incorporated, remove the pan from the heat and set aside to cool for about 20 minutes.

When cool, stir two thirds (6 ounces) of the goat cheese into the mixture.

Using a small, sharp knife, cut a generous pocket about 1 inch across in the thickest side of each breast, being careful not to cut all the way through. Wiggle the knife slightly inside the chicken to open the pocket.

Stuff each pocket with the spinach mixture and secure the opening of the pockets with small metal or wooden skewers.

In a large sauté pan, heat the remaining 2 tablespoons olive oil over high heat and, when very hot, cook the chicken breasts, skin side down, for about 2 minutes or until the skin is golden brown. Turn the breasts over and cook for about 2 minutes longer. You will have to do this in batches. Add more oil if needed.

Transfer the breasts, skin side up, to a shallow baking pan large enough to hold them in a single layer, and bake for about 30 minutes or until cooked through and an instant-read thermometer registers 170°F when inserted in the thickest part of the breast meat (not the filling). Remove the pan from the oven and transfer the chicken to a cutting board. Let the breasts rest for about 5 minutes.

Meanwhile, make the sauce: Drain all but 1 tablespoon of the oil from the sauté pan and set it over medium heat. Add the shallots and the remaining clove garlic and sauté for about 1 minute or until softened.

Add the wine and raise the heat to high. Bring to a boil and cook for about 4 minutes or until syrupy. Stir in the cream, reduce the heat to medium, and cook for 5 to 6 minutes or until reduced by half.

Stir in the remaining one third goat cheese and the remaining tablespoon basil and reduce the heat to low. Cook gently, stirring, until smooth. Stir in the chicken base, season to taste with salt and pepper, and cook for about 1 minute until well blended.

Slice each breast into 6 to 8 slices for serving. Arrange the chicken on each of 4 serving plates and spoon the sauce down both sides of the plate.

NOTE: You may have to ask the butcher to bone the whole breasts for you, as these are not familiar cuts in the supermarket. Be sure to ask him to leave the skin on the breasts. Each breast will weigh 12 to 14 ounces after boning. If the breasts weigh a little more or less, adjust the cooking time accordingly.

SAUTÉED DUCK BREASTS
with Port and Garlic

If you have never cooked duck, don't wait any longer. Duck is rich and full bodied and as such is a real treat. It's fattier than most poultry, but during cooking most of the fat is rendered and spooned from the pan in this recipe. The skin gets crispy as it cooks, so watch the temperature of the heat under the pan so that the skin does not burn, and the meat never cooks beyond medium. Slice the duck breasts and serve them with the sauce for an elegant and yet quite simple dish. **SERVES 4**

Four 12- to 14-ounce duck breasts, excess fat
    trimmed, duck skin intact

2 ounces (4 tablespoons) Glace de Canard Gold
    duck stock base, see Note

5 cups hot water

2 tablespoons unsalted butter

6 large cloves garlic, thinly sliced

1 cup port wine

1 tablespoon all-purpose flour

Kosher salt and freshly ground black pepper

1 tablespoon peanut oil

Chopped fresh flat-leaf parsley, for serving

WINE RECOMMENDATION
Cabernet Francs from the Loire Valley, specifically Chinon, are light and refreshing enough to allow the flavor of the duck to shine through. They also have a light acidity to balance the sweetness of the port sauce and the lush texture of the duck. Our suggestion is Domaine Bernard Baudry from Chinon in the Loire Valley of France.

Remove the duck breasts from the refrigerator and let them rest at room temperature for 30 to 60 minutes.

To make the sauce: In a saucepan, stir the duck stock base into the hot water until it dissolves. Set the pan over high heat and bring to a boil. Boil for about 25 minutes or until reduced to 1 cup.

In a large nonreactive skillet, melt 1 tablespoon of the butter over medium-low heat. Add the sliced garlic and sauté for about 2 minutes or until golden. Add the port, raise the heat to medium, and bring to a boil. Boil, uncovered, for about 5 minutes.

Add the reduced duck stock and boil for 8 to 10 minutes or until reduced to 1 cup.

In a small bowl, mix the remaining tablespoon of butter with the flour into a paste. Whisk this into the sauce until incorporated. Let the sauce simmer for about 1 minute or until

recipe continues on next page

thickened. Season to taste with salt and pepper, cover, and keep warm over very low heat.

To cook the duck: Pat the duck breasts with paper towels and then season with salt and pepper.

In a medium sauté pan, heat the oil over medium-high heat. (You might want to use 2 pans and cook 2 breasts in each pan.) Reduce the heat to medium and cook the breasts, skin side down, for 5 to 8 minutes, or until golden brown. Spoon excess fat from the pan and discard. Turn the breasts over and cook for about 7 minutes longer. Continue removing the fat as the duck cooks.

Remove the breasts from the pan and let them rest on a cutting board for about 2 minutes. The skin should be beautifully browned and crispy and the meat will be medium (still a little pink).

Slice each breast crosswise on an angle into ½-inch-thick slices and put on a warm plate. Spoon the sauce along both sides of the breast meat and garnish with chopped parsley.

NOTE: Duck base stock is sold in 1½-ounce packages, so you might choose to use only one or to use two and have some left over. More Than Gourmet's Glace de Canard Gold can be ordered online.

ᔓ CELEBRITY CLIP ᔓ

MORTON'S PROVIDES its guests with one-of-a-kind special events. One such occasion is the partnership with ESPN AM 1000 radio for a series we call "Lunch with a Legend," in our hometown of Chicago. The series combines Chicagoland sports icons with our legendary food and drinks for what is called "a prime slice of the good life." Featured legends have included former Cubs great Ryne Sandberg; John Paxson, general manager of the Chicago Bulls; John McDonough, president of the Chicago Blackhawks; Brent Musburger, ESPN and ABC sports commentator; Jerry Reinsdorf, chairman of the Chicago White Sox and the Chicago Bulls; and current Cubs player Mark DeRosa. These events provide our guests with a matchless dining experience as the private boardroom at Morton's transforms into a live, on-air radio studio. Here's a quote from Brent Musburger during one of our broadcasts: "When you come to Morton's, you can always count on the quality, whether you're in Columbus, Ohio, or down where I am in West Palm Beach. It is truly one of the restaurants that has never lost its class and ability to serve great food." We could not have said it any better! ᔓ

AMERICAN BARBECUE MENU,
MORTON'S STYLE

BARBECUED BABY BACK RIBS, PAGE 159

COLORADO BEEF BRISKET, PAGE 138

MORTON'S ASIAN SLAW, PAGE 62

TOMATO, MOZZARELLA, AND PROSCIUTTO SALAD, PAGE 57

―――――――

KEY LIME MARGARITA, PAGE 17

PORT SANGRIA, PAGE 24

GRILLED SHRIMP WITH RED PEPPER BUERRE BLANC

FISH AND SEAFOOD

SALMON FILLET WITH SAUTÉED
SPINACH

—

Larry King's Favorite
CHEF CHRIS ROOK'S SWORDFISH

—

BROCHETTES OF SWORDFISH

—

GRILLED SEA BASS

—

GRILLED NORTHWEST HALIBUT

Troy Aikman's Favorite
SEARED SESAME-CRUSTED TUNA WITH
SOY-GINGER SAUCE

—

GRILLED SHRIMP WITH RED PEPPER
BEURRE BLANC

—

BAKED SEA SCALLOPS WITH
BEURRE BLANC

—

TEMPURA LOBSTER TAIL

SALMON FILLET
WITH SAUTÉED SPINACH

Our customers in the Pacific Northwest demand wild, line-caught salmon—and nothing else—for this and any other salmon dish we serve. Who can blame them? Wild salmon tastes markedly better than farmed salmon, and so if you find it in your market, buy it for this magnificent dish. Like most of our fish and seafood recipes, this is equally successful as a first course when the portions are reduced. For this recipe we have to thank Dominque Place, who with his wife, ChouChou, owned G & D Seafood, the company in Woodinville, Washington, that makes our smoked salmon.

SERVES 4

SEASONING MIX

1 teaspoon fennel seeds

1 teaspoon minced garlic

1 tablespoon chopped fresh flat-leaf parsley

1 teaspoon sweet paprika

1 teaspoon salt

⅛ teaspoon freshly ground white pepper

BASIL BUTTER

1½ ounces fresh basil leaves, large leaves torn into pieces (approximately 2 cups)

Juice of 1 lime

8 tablespoons (1 stick) unsalted butter, softened

SALMON

Four 4- by 2-inch pieces frozen puff pastry, thawed

1 large egg yolk whisked with 1 teaspoon cold water

1½ cups Chardonnay or other dry white wine

1 tablespoon finely chopped shallots

1 cup heavy cream

3 tablespoons olive oil

6 to 8 ounces baby spinach (about 8 cups)

Salt and freshly ground black pepper

4 skinless salmon fillets, each about 6 ounces

WINE RECOMMENDATION
Gavi is made from the Cortese grape and is a great alternative to Chardonnay with almond, orange, and grapefruit and a crisp minerality. We like Principessa Gavia Gavi from Piedmont, Italy.

A California Pinot Noir would work equally well with this complex dish. Try Hope and Grace Pinot Noir from the Sleepy Holly Vineyard .

To make the seasoning mix: In a small bowl, stir together the fennel, garlic, parsley, paprika, salt, and white pepper.

To make the basil butter: In the bowl of a food processor fitted with a metal blade, pulse the basil leaves with the lime juice and a pinch of the seasoning mix until the leaves are nicely chopped. Scrape the herb mixture into the softened butter and mix until blended. You could chop the basil leaves and mix this butter by hand, if you prefer. Set aside at room temperature.

recipe continues on page 174

To cook the salmon: Preheat the oven to 425°F.

Arrange the puff pastry rectangles about 2 inches apart on a baking sheet lined with parchment paper. Brush each rectangle with the egg yolk mixture and let it dry. Bake for 10 to 15 minutes or until the pastry is puffed and golden brown. Carefully transfer the puff pastry to wire racks to cool.

When cool enough to handle, split the rectangles crosswise into a top and a bottom and set aside.

Reduce the oven temperature to 375°F.

In a medium nonreactive saucepan, bring the wine and shallots to a boil over medium-high heat. Cook at a rapid simmer for 12 to 15 minutes or until reduced and syrupy (you will have about 3 tablespoons). Stir the cream into the pan and bring to a simmer. Reduce the heat to medium and cook for about 15 minutes or until reduced by half. Swirl the pan once or twice.

In a medium sauté pan set over high heat, heat 1 tablespoon of the olive oil and add the spinach. Cook for about 30 seconds, stirring. Season with salt and pepper, stir in 2 tablespoons of the basil butter, and cook for about 30 seconds longer or until the spinach wilts. Cover with a lid to keep warm.

Drain any liquid from the spinach.

Remove the sauce from the heat. Add the remaining 6 tablespoons of basil butter to the sauce, about 2 tablespoons at a time, whisking constantly until the butter is incorporated so that the sauce does not separate. Wait until the butter blends with the sauce before adding the next amount. When all the butter is incorporated, the sauce will be silky and thick enough to coat a spoon lightly. Season with about 1 teaspoon of the seasoning mix. Set aside, covered.

Rub both sides of the salmon fillets with about 2 tablespoons of olive oil and then with the remaining seasoning mix. Lay the fillets in a baking pan and, depending on the thickness of the fillets, bake for 8 to 12 minutes or until just cooked through. The salmon will be moist in the center.

Set the bottom half of each rectangle of puff pastry on each of 4 serving plates. Top each with spinach and then a salmon fillet. Drizzle the sauce around the plate and on the salmon and then sandwich the salmon with the top half of the puff pastry rectangles. Serve immediately with any extra sauce passed on the side.

CHEF CHRIS ROOK'S SWORDFISH

When executive chef Chris Rook and Donna Rundle, who is manager of restaurant services, joined me in my home kitchen to test recipes for the book, both Donna and I were skeptical when Chris breaded swordfish and put the fish in the oven. We were immediate and passionate converts when we tasted it. The fish was exceptionally juicy and tender—and so easy to prepare. Our swordfish has long been a favorite of media mogul and the "King" of interviews, Larry King. **SERVES 4**

Four 8- to 10-ounce swordfish steaks, each 1¼ to 1½ inches thick

Salt and freshly ground white pepper

½ cup all-purpose flour

2 large eggs

1½ cups Tuscan Bread Crumbs, page 226

2 tablespoons olive oil

2 lemons, halved, for serving

WINE RECOMMENDATION

Cru Beaujolais from France has the unique ability to fill your mouth without being heavy. This characteristic makes it a perfect accompaniment to a dish such as this. Notes of fresh red and black fruits blend well with the Parmesan and the meaty swordfish. We like Georges Duboeuf Fleurie from Beaujolais.

A mildly oaked Chardonnay from California is strong enough to match the richness of the swordfish without overpowering the delicate flavors of the bread crumbs. Try Iron Horse Estate Chardonnay from Green Valley, California.

Preheat the oven to 400°F.

Lightly season the swordfish steaks with salt and pepper and dust each with flour.

Whisk the eggs and 2 tablespoons water in a shallow bowl and put the bread crumbs in another bowl.

Dip the swordfish steaks in the egg to coat on both sides and let any excess drip off. Dip them in the bread crumbs so that they are completely coated.

In a large, oven-safe nonstick sauté pan, heat the olive oil. Sauté the swordfish steaks for about 2 minutes on each side, or until golden brown.

Transfer to the oven and bake for 5 to 6 minutes. Turn carefully and bake for 5 to 6 minutes longer or until cooked through and the fish flakes. Garnish with fresh lemon halves and serve immediately.

BROCHETTES OF SWORDFISH

This is a tasty one-dish meal made with swordfish, potatoes, and zucchini that is completed with the compote and sauce. This is wonderful in the summertime when you fire up the grill. **SERVE 4**

COMPOTE

1 large leek

3 tablespoons extra-virgin olive oil

3 large tomatoes, peeled and seeded (see Note, page 124), and finely chopped (about 3 cups)

1 teaspoon fennel seeds

Salt and freshly ground black pepper

SWORDFISH

⅓ cup extra-virgin olive oil

Juice of 1 large lemon

3 tablespoons light soy sauce

18 ounces skinned swordfish steaks, cut into 16 large cubes (each about 1½ inches square)

VINAIGRETTE

½ cup extra-virgin olive oil

¼ cup balsamic vinegar

¼ teaspoon salt

⅛ teaspoon freshly ground black pepper

¼ teaspoon fresh lemon juice

VEGETABLES

Vegetable oil cooking spray

8 small red potatoes, halved (about 12 ounces)

1 medium or 4 small zucchini, sliced into ½-inch-thick rounds

Kosher salt and freshly ground black pepper

Chopped fresh flat-leaf parsley, for serving

WINE RECOMMENDATION
A lightly oaked Chardonnay from California brings out the richness of the swordfish and blends well with the leeks. We suggest Cakebread or Napa.

COCKTAIL RECOMMENDATION
Americano Cocktail, page 20

To prepare the compote: Trim all but 2 inches of the green part of the leek. Chop the leek into small dice; you should have about 1 cup. Rinse the diced leek under running water to remove all sand and grit. Drain well.

In a large skillet, heat the olive oil over low heat. Add the leek and sauté for 1 to 2 minutes, or until it starts to soften. Add the tomatoes and fennel seeds, stir to mix, and then season to taste with salt and pepper.

Raise the heat slightly and bring the contents of the pan to a low simmer. Simmer, partially covered, for 25 to 30 minutes, or until the tomato liquid evaporates and the compote thickens. Adjust the heat up or down to maintain the simmer.

Let the compote cool before using, or transfer to a lidded container and refrigerate for up to 24 hours. You will have about 2½ cups of compote. Let the compote reach room temperature before serving.

To prepare the swordfish: In a shallow bowl, whisk together the olive oil, lemon juice, and soy sauce. Add the swordfish cubes and toss gently to coat. Cover and refrigerate for at least 30 minutes and up to 2 hours. Do not leave the fish in the marinade for any longer or it will toughen.

Put 4 long wooden skewers in a shallow pan filled with warm tap water. Let them soak for at least 1 hour so that they don't scorch. If you use metal skewers, they do not need soaking.

To make the vinaigrette: In a small bowl, whisk the oil with the vinegar until emulsified. Season with the salt and pepper and then whisk in the lemon juice. Adjust the salt and pepper. Set aside.

To cook the brochettes and vegetables: Prepare a charcoal or gas grill or preheat the boiler and position a rack about 4 inches from the heating element. Before igniting the grill, lightly spray the grill rack with cooking spray. The coals should be medium-hot for the charcoal grill. The burners should be on high for the gas grill.

In a small saucepan, bring about 3 cups of salted water to a boil and cook the potatoes for about 12 minutes or until nearly cooked through but still offering some resistance when pierced with a sharp knife. Scoop out the potatoes with a slotted spoon and set aside to cool.

In the same saucepan, boil the zucchini for about 45 seconds. Drain and set aside to cool.

Lift the cubed swordfish from the marinade and begin to make the brochettes. Thread the skewers with a potato half, zucchini round, and swordfish cube. Repeat the pattern on the 4 skewers until all the food is used. Drizzle a little marinade over the skewers. Discard the remaining marinade.

Sprinkle the brochettes with salt and pepper and grill or broil for 4 to 6 minutes until the swordfish is nicely browned yet moist in the center. Do not overcook.

Spoon 2 to 3 tablespoons of the compote down the center of each serving plate. Top with a brochette and drizzle with vinaigrette. Garnish with parsley and serve.

GRILLED SEA BASS

This light dish is easily cooked on the grill or under the broiler and then served with the pineapple chutney. We find that fish served with fruit chutneys is especially easy and satisfying: The chutney adds intense, fresh flavor. Please use fresh pineapple; it is easy to find these days. **SERVES 4**

½ cup diced fresh pineapple

¼ cup diced red onion

¼ cup seeded and diced plum tomato

1½ teaspoons minced jalapeño pepper

1½ teaspoons chopped fresh cilantro

⅛ teaspoon salt

⅛ teaspoon freshly ground black pepper

Vegetable oil cooking spray, for the grill rack if using

¼ cup extra-virgin olive oil

1 teaspoon seasoned salt

Four 8- to 10-ounce pieces sea bass or similar flaky, white fish such as grouper, cod, or halibut, each 1½ to 2 inches thick

WINE RECOMMENDATION
Think halfway between Sauvignon Blanc and Riesling and you will come up with Grüner Veltliner. This grape has sweetness and acidity to balance the fruit and the dish's heat, but the acidity brings out the best texture and flavor of the fatty sea bass. Perhaps something produced by Laurenz V., "Charming," Grüner Veltliner, Kamptal, Niederösterreich, Austria.

BEER RECOMMENDATION
Negra Modelo, a Vienna-style beer from Mexico, is a sweet malt with brown sugar and caramel flavors that balance the acidity and the heat of the chutney while being bold enough to stand up to the sea bass.

In a small bowl, gently stir together the pineapple, red onion, tomato, jalapeño pepper, cilantro, salt, and pepper. Cover and refrigerate for at least 1 hour and up to 3 hours to allow the flavors to blend.

Prepare a charcoal or gas grill or preheat the broiler and position a rack about 4 inches from the heating element. Before igniting the grill, lightly spray the grill rack with vegetable oil spray. The coals should be medium hot for the charcoal grill. The burners should be on medium-high for the gas grill.

In a shallow plate or pie dish, whisk together the olive oil and seasoned salt. Dip each fillet in the oil and turn to coat. Grill or broil for 3 to 5 minutes, depending on the thickness of the fish. Carefully turn and cook the other side for 3 to 5 minutes longer or until the fish is cooked all the way through and flakes.

To serve, spoon about ¼ cup of the chutney over each piece of sea bass.

GRILLED NORTHWEST HALIBUT

Here is another easy grilled fish jazzed up with a fresh salsa. The tangerine salsa, with its hint of heat, perfectly complements any firm, white fish and adds color to every dish. **SERVES 4**

TANGERINE SALSA

6 tangerines

1 serrano chile, minced (about ¾ tablespoon)

¼ cup finely chopped roasted red bell pepper

¼ cup finely chopped shallots (about 4 shallots)

3 tablespoons fresh lime juice

2 tablespoons extra-virgin olive oil

1½ tablespoons finely chopped fresh chives

2 teaspoons chopped fresh flat-leaf parsley

½ tablespoon chopped fresh cilantro

⅛ teaspoon salt

⅛ teaspoon freshly ground black pepper

HALIBUT

Four 6-ounce halibut fillets, or similar flaky, white fish such as sea bass, grouper, or cod

Vegetable oil cooking spray, for the grill rack

1 tablespoon vegetable oil

¼ teaspoon kosher salt

¼ teaspoon freshly ground black pepper

WINE RECOMMENDATION
Gewürztraminer from Alsace has a fruity and acidic balance that blends well with the heat and fruit of the salsa. The full mouthfeel of this wine showcases the flavor of the halibut. Our choice is Albert Mann.

To prepare the salsa: Extract and strain the juice from 4 of the tangerines. You should have about ¾ cup of juice. Transfer the juice to a small nonreactive saucepan and bring to a boil over high heat. Reduce the heat and simmer for 6 to 8 minutes or until the liquid reduces by half and the flavors concentrate. Set aside to cool.

Peel the remaining 2 tangerines, divide them into segments, and add them to the juice. Stir in the chile, roasted red pepper, shallots, lime juice, olive oil, chives, parsley, cilantro, salt, and pepper and mix well.

To cook the fish: Prepare a charcoal or gas grill or preheat the broiler and position a rack about 4 inches from the heating element. Before igniting the grill, lightly spray the grill rack with vegetable oil spray. The coals should be medium hot for the charcoal grill. The burners should be on medium-high for the gas grill.

Brush the fish with the oil and season each fillet with salt and pepper. Grill or broil the fish for 3 to 5 minutes or until lightly golden. Carefully turn the fillets over and grill for 3 to 5 minutes longer until cooked through and the fish flakes.

Divide the salsa among 4 serving plates. Put a fish fillet on top of the salsa.

SEARED SESAME-CRUSTED TUNA
WITH SOY-GINGER SAUCE

Dallas Cowboy superstar and Hall of Fame quarterback, Troy Aikman, is regarded as one of the greatest NFL quarterbacks of all time. He led his team to three Super Bowl victories. He also knows a great seafood dish when he tries one. This tuna is one of his favorites. **SERVES 6**

SAUCE

¾ cup soy sauce

½ cup white rice wine vinegar

1 tablespoon sesame oil

1½ teaspoons minced peeled fresh ginger

1½ teaspoons finely minced garlic

1 teaspoon crushed red pepper flakes

TUNA

Six 10-ounce tuna steaks, each about 1 inch thick

¼ cup white sesame seeds

¼ cup black sesame seeds

Kosher salt and freshly ground black pepper

½ cup sesame oil

2 teaspoons wasabi paste

1 lemon, quartered

4 sprigs flat-leaf parsley

WINE RECOMMENDATION

As are many Asian-inspired dishes, this is best paired with an off-dry Riesling from Pfalz or Mosel Saar Ruwer. I like a great Riesling on the market now called Saint M from Pfalz, which is quite inexpensive and hails from the famous Loosen family. It will cut the soy and ginger and offset the sweetness of the fish. A perfect pairing.

To make the sauce, whisk together the soy sauce, vinegar, and sesame oil. Add the ginger, garlic, and pepper flakes and stir to mix. Set aside.

To cook the tuna: In a shallow dish large enough to hold a tuna steak, mix together the white and black sesame seeds.

Season both sides of the tuna steaks with salt and pepper. One at a time, put the tuna steaks in the sesame seeds, pressing them into the fish to adhere. Turn the steak over and press the seeds into the other side to distribute evenly.

In a large sauté pan, heat the oil over medium-high heat. When the oil is hot, sear the tuna steaks for about 1 minute on each side. Using tongs, hold the tuna upright to brown the edges in the hot oil and until the tuna steaks are medium-rare. For more well-done tuna, increase the cooking time by 30 to 60 seconds on each side.

Lay a tuna steak on each of 4 serving plates. Spread a little wasabi paste on each lemon quarter. Garnish with a lemon quarter and parsley sprig. Serve the sauce on the side.

GRILLED SHRIMP
with Red Pepper Beurre Blanc

This is an elegant first course or indulgent main course and so easy to make, particularly if you already have the beurre blanc on hand. Nothing could be simpler than mixing the roasted peppers with the sauce in anticipation of serving it with the shrimp once they are broiled. **SERVES 2 OR 3 AS AN ENTRÉE; 6 AS A FIRST COURSE**

2 large red bell peppers
1½ cups warm Beurre Blanc, page 230
Vegetable oil cooking spray

12 large raw shrimp (21–25 count), peeled and deveined, shells reserved
Chopped fresh flat-leaf parsley, for serving

WINE RECOMMENDATION
The flinty, lemony characteristics of Chardonnay grapes from France's Chablis region elevate all of the flavors of this dish. We suggest Dauvissat-Camus Les Preuses Grand Cru.

The crisp peach, honey, and almond flavors of a Pinot Grigio from California play well, too. Try Swanson Pinot Grigio from Napa.

Preheat the broiler. Submerge 6 wooden skewers in a shallow dish of cold water to soak for at least 30 minutes.

Char the peppers under the hot broiler until they blister and are blackened on all sides. Rotate them as they cook to char evenly. Remove the peppers from the heat and transfer them to a plastic or paper bag. Close the bag and let the peppers steam for about 5 minutes. Rub the blackened skin from the peppers. Hold them under cold, running water and rub any burned pieces from the vegetables, if necessary. Make a slit along 1 side of the peppers, lay them on a work surface, and scrape out the seeds and membrane. Remove and discard the stems. Cut the peppers into several pieces, transfer to a broiler-safe dish, and reheat just until warm.

In a 1-quart stainless-steel bowl, mix the beurre blanc with the peppers, and with an immersion blender or hand-held electric mixer, mix for about 10 seconds just until the sauce is pink and small pieces of peppers are visible. Set the bowl over a larger one filled with hot water to keep the sauce warm.

Lightly spray a broiler pan with cooking spray. Thread 2 or 3 shrimp on each skewer and lay them on the pan. Cook about 4 inches from the heat for about 2 minutes on each side or until the shrimp turn pink and firm.

Meanwhile, spoon the sauce onto each of 6 small plates or a single platter.

Slide the shrimp from the skewers and put 2 on each plate on top of the sauce (or put them all on top of the sauce on the platter). Garnish with chopped parsley.

BAKED SEA SCALLOPS
WITH BEURRE BLANC

I am very fond of both scallops and leeks, and the light flavors go well together. When you see fresh scallops, particularly those called diver scallops, grab them. These are the scallops that are hand fished—divers actually dive for them—and they tend to taste better, fresher, and cleaner. We serve this both as a main course and as a first course. Either way, it's superb. **SERVES 4 AS AN ENTRÉE; 6 AS FIRST COURSE**

2 leeks

1½ teaspoons unsalted butter

Salt and freshly ground white pepper

1¼ cups warm Beurre Blanc, page 230

Vegetable oil cooking spray

1 pound large scallops (12 to 15 scallops)

WINE RECOMMENDATION
The melon and citrus characteristics of Oregon Pinot Gris make it a good fit with the mild acidity of the wine to balance the richness of the scallops. We recommend Ponzi Vineyard's Pinot Gris from the Willamette Valley in Oregon.

New Zealand Sauvignon Blancs have an herbaceous quality that balances the flavors of the beurre blanc and brings the texture and flavor of the scallops to the forefront. Try Cloudy Bay Sauvignon Blanc from Marlborough, New Zealand.

Preheat the oven to 450°F.

Trim the root end and the stiff green ends of the leek. Split it lengthwise, white and light green parts, and rinse it under cold running water to remove any sand or dirt. Slice the leek crosswise into very thin slices. You should have about ½ cup of sliced leeks.

In a small sauté pan, melt the butter over very low heat. Add the leeks, cover, and cook for about 6 minutes. Remove the cover and cook for 3 to 4 minutes longer or until tender. Season lightly with salt and pepper.

Put the warm beurre blanc in a stainless-steel bowl.

Transfer the leeks to the beurre blanc. Set the bowl over a larger one filled with hot water to keep warm.

Spray a baking pan large enough to hold the scallops in a single layer with cooking spray. Spread the scallops in a single layer and bake for about 5 minutes, turning once, or until opaque and barely cooked through.

Divide the sauce among 4 small plates and top the sauce with 3 scallops on each plate. Serve immediately.

TEMPURA LOBSTER TAIL

When you want an indulgent, sublime treat, fry up a couple of tempura-style lobster tails. You can make this with fresh or frozen lobster tails, which means you can use this recipe all year long. It looks impressive and tastes even better; and while you can serve this with an elegant frisée or mesclun salad, it also tastes very good with Morton's Asian Slaw, page 62, or a bowl of crispy potato chips. **SERVES 4**

WASABI MAYONNAISE

½ cup mayonnaise

1 tablespoon wasabi powder

1 tablespoon fresh lemon juice

¼ teaspoon kosher salt

LOBSTER TAILS

Four 8- to 10-ounce Australian, Maine, or other
    lobster tails (thawed completely if frozen)

2 cups ice water

2 large egg yolks

¼ cup sesame oil

4 teaspoons wasabi powder

1 teaspoon kosher salt

1 teaspoon freshly ground black pepper

1 cup plus 2 tablespoons all-purpose flour

½ cup cornstarch

Vegetable oil, for frying

WINE RECOMMENDATION
The sweet nature of Riesling from Australia works well with the heat of the wasabi, but the acidity brings out the best texture and flavors of the tempura lobster and the rich mayonnaise. We recommend Penfolds Bin 51 Riesling from Eden Valley in the Barossa Ranges of South Australia.

COCKTAIL RECOMMENDATION
Pomegranate-Sake Cocktail, page 20

To make the wasabi mayonnaise: In a small bowl, stir together the mayonnaise, wasabi powder, lemon juice, and salt. When well blended, cover and refrigerate.

To cook the lobster: Using sturdy scissors, carefully cut the top of the lobster shell down the middle to the tail. Make a second cut across the last section of tail shell to form a T-shaped cut. Try not to cut into the lobster meat.

Remove the meat from the shell and leave it attached to the "T" end of the shell. Thread an 8- to 10-inch wooden skewer through the length of the lobster meat. Thread a second skewer parallel to the first. This will keep the tail straight during cooking. Put the tail in a large, shallow pan and repeat the process with the remaining lobster tails. Cover with a kitchen towel or plastic wrap and refrigerate.

In a mixing bowl, whisk together the ice water, egg yolks, sesame oil, wasabi powder, salt, and pepper.

In a metal bowl, whisk together the flour and cornstarch. Sift this mixture over the water and egg mixture, whisking constantly to blend the dry ingredients into the liquid. The batter will be thin; the consistency of buttermilk. Submerge the bowl in a larger one filled with cold water and ice cubes. Take care not to get any more water in the batter. The batter must be kept cold.

Pour enough oil into a deep heavy pot to fill it to a depth of 4 to 5 inches. The pan should be large enough to hold a lobster tail easily and the oil deep enough to cover the tail.

Set the oil over medium-high heat and let the oil heat to 375°F on a deep-fat frying thermometer. If you have a deep-fat fryer, use it.

Dip the meat portion only of the lobster tail into the batter to coat it completely. Repeat with another tail. Carefully submerge the tails into the hot oil using tongs. Fry for 8 to 10 minutes or until golden.

Very carefully lift the tails from the hot oil and let them drain on paper towels.

Let the oil regain its temperature and fry the remaining 2 tails.

Serve immediately with the wasabi mayonnaise.

BAKED ONIONS WITH GRUYÈRE

SIDE DISHES

BAKED ONIONS WITH GRUYÈRE

—

SAUTÉED GARLIC GREEN BEANS

—

BAKED TOMATOES WITH
GORGONZOLA

—

SPINACH-STUFFED TOMATOES

—

ROASTED BUTTERNUT SQUASH

ROASTED FINGERLING POTATOES

—

BLUE-CHEESE FRENCH FRIES

—

TWICE-BAKED POTATOES

—

D.L. Hughley's Favorite
MACARONI AND CHEESE

BAKED ONIONS
WITH GRUYÈRE

When onions are baked they turn sweet and juicy, and when you start with sweet onions, they are especially luscious. Yet, even if you only have sharp yellow onions, the dish will be delightful and echo the warm, rich notes of onion soup. Plus, the sage boosts the flavor in marvelous ways. While you can make these ahead of time, reheat them in the oven so that the cheese is hot and meltingly yummy. **SERVES 10**

Vegetable oil cooking spray
5 medium sweet white onions, such as Vidalia
2 teaspoons extra-virgin olive oil
Salt and freshly ground black pepper
1 cup low-sodium beef broth, see Note

2 teaspoons low-sodium soy sauce
1 cup finely shredded Gruyère cheese (4 ounces)
2 teaspoons finely chopped fresh sage

Preheat the oven to 400°F. Spray a large, shallow baking dish with cooking spray. The baking dish should be large enough to hold 10 onion halves.

Cut about ¼ inch off the top and bottom of the onions so that the halves will be able to sit on a plate. Cut the onions in half at the equator and then peel them. Arrange the onion halves, cut sides up, in the baking dish.

Brush the exposed tops of the onions with olive oil and sprinkle with salt and pepper. Bake for about 35 minutes.

In a glass measuring cup, mix together the beef broth and soy sauce and pour this over the onions. Continue baking the onions for about 1 hour longer, basting occasionally. If the liquid evaporates, add a little water.

Sprinkle the cheese and sage evenly over the onion halves. Bake for 5 to 7 minutes more or until the cheese melts.

NOTE: If you use regular beef broth, not low-sodium broth, omit the salt from the recipe.

SAUTÉED GARLIC GREEN BEANS

These green beans are one of our most popular side dishes. They are simply elegant and easy to make. Start with fresh green beans, topped and tailed (translation: Snap off the tapered ends), and then shock them in ice water after blanching to keep them bright green. **SERVES 4**

1 pound fresh haricots verts or slender green
   beans

3 tablespoons unsalted butter

1 tablespoon finely chopped shallot (about
   1 small shallot)

1 tablespoon minced garlic

Salt and freshly ground white pepper

Set a large bowl filled with water and ice cubes near the stove. In a large pot partly filled with salted, boiling water, cook the beans for 2 to 3 minutes until bright green. Drain and plunge into the ice water to stop the cooking. Drain thoroughly.

In a large sauté pan, melt the butter over medium heat until bubbling. Add the shallot and garlic and cook for about 30 seconds or just until softened.

Add the beans, toss a few times, and season with salt and pepper. Sauté for about 2 minutes longer or until heated through. Serve immediately.

⤳ CELEBRITY CLIP ⤳

ONE OF HOLLYWOOD'S most versatile and talented film stars, Leonardo DiCaprio, has visited Morton's many times over the years, and recently he and Israeli supermodel girlfriend Bar Refaeli were at Morton's in Beverly Hills. The couple was joined by DiCaprio's manager and his date and they chatted over Shrimp Alexander and Oysters as an appetizer. DiCaprio kicked off his meal with the Beefsteak Tomato Salad and shared the porterhouse with his girlfriend, along with Sautéed Wild Mushrooms, Creamed Spinach, Lyonnaise Potatoes, and one of DiCaprio's favorites, our Morton's Legendary Hot Chocolate Cake. ⤳

BAKED TOMATOES
WITH GORGONZOLA

When you pair this with grilled steak, its flavors explode. It also adds great color and interest to the plate. I came up with the idea when I was scouring my kitchen, looking for something easy that would taste good with beef, and noticed I had both tomatoes and Gorgonzola on hand. This is best with garden-ripe tomatoes at their peak of summertime goodness, but any decent tomato will work well, as the fruit sweetens as it bakes. Use the pre-crumbled Gorgonzola if you find it easier, although this tastes best with the very finest blue cheese you can find, crumbled by hand over the tomatoes. **SERVES 6**

3 medium ripe tomatoes, cored
About 2 teaspoons garlic salt
Freshly ground black pepper

6 teaspoons dry bread crumbs
6 teaspoons crumbled Gorgonzola cheese

Preheat the oven to 375°F.

Cut each tomato in half crosswise and set in a baking pan large enough to hold them snugly. If necessary, slice a little off the bottom of the tomatoes so that they sit in the dish without wobbling.

Sprinkle each tomato half with garlic salt and a turn of the peppermill. Sprinkle each with 1 teaspoon of bread crumbs and 1 teaspoon of cheese.

Bake the tomatoes for about 5 minutes and then remove from the oven.

Turn on the broiler and broil the tomatoes for a minute or two or until the cheese melts.

SPINACH-STUFFED TOMATOES

The toughest part of making these superb stuffed tomatoes is blanching and drying the spinach. Once you get that done, the rest is a breeze. Start with good, big red or yellow tomatoes, which when stuffed with the spinach are pretty and colorful. And they taste great. **SERVES 6**

12 ounces fresh spinach leaves

4 tablespoons (½ stick) unsalted butter

1 tablespoon finely chopped shallot (about 1 small shallot)

Pinch of sugar

Salt and freshly ground white pepper

3 large tomatoes, cored

2 tablespoons freshly grated Parmesan cheese

Preheat the oven to 500°F.

Set a large bowl filled with water and ice cubes near the stove. In a large saucepan partly filled with lightly salted boiling water, cook the spinach for about 20 seconds or until just wilted. Stir well and then lift the spinach from the boiling water and immediately submerge in the ice water to stop the cooking. Lift the spinach from the ice water, let the spinach drain as much as possible, and squeeze dry. You will have about 2 cups of spinach.

In a medium saucepan, heat the butter over medium-low heat until bubbling. Add the shallot and cook for about 3 minutes, stirring, until softened. Add the spinach and sugar, season with salt and pepper, and cook for about 1 minute or just until the spinach is hot and nicely coated with the butter and the shallot is evenly distributed. Set aside to cool.

Cut each tomato in half across the equator. Scoop out the seeds and center meat to make a "bowl." Cut a thin slice from the bottom of each half so each sits level on a rimmed baking sheet or shallow baking pan.

Season the tomatoes with salt and pepper and then divide the spinach evenly among the 6 halves. Sprinkle each with the cheese.

Bake for 10 to 12 minutes or until the tomatoes are heated through and the cheese melts. Serve right away.

ROASTED BUTTERNUT SQUASH

The squash and sage come together to say "fall and winter," and I look forward to making this dish as the days grow shorter and cooler and the Chicago winds pick up. My friends have come to expect it among the many side dishes on the Thanksgiving table, and I wouldn't dream of disappointing them. **SERVES 6**

About 2 pounds butternut squash (1 squash), peeled and seeded, flesh cut into 1-inch cubes

¾ cup thinly sliced yellow onion (1 small onion)

6 whole cloves garlic, peeled

2 tablespoons olive oil

2 tablespoons chopped fresh rosemary leaves

2 tablespoons chopped fresh sage leaves

1 teaspoon salt

¼ teaspoon freshly ground black pepper

In a large mixing bowl, toss together the squash cubes, onion, garlic cloves, olive oil, rosemary, sage, salt, and pepper.

Spread the mixture in a large, shallow baking pan, cover with plastic wrap, and let marinate at room temperature for about 2 hours.

Preheat the oven to 450°F.

Remove the plastic wrap and roast the squash for 20 to 25 minutes, turning once or twice with a large spatula to encourage even browning and cooking. The squash is cooked when it is browned and very tender. Serve hot.

☙ CELEBRITY CLIP ☙

DUE TO THE huge success of her Disney show *Hannah Montana*, Miley Cyrus has become a teen sensation and sells out to audiences all over the world. On her "Best of Both Worlds" tour stop in Washington, D.C., Ms. Cyrus dined at Morton's in Georgetown on a Sunday night, dressing up in a fancy red dress and sharing a double-cut filet and assorted side dishes with two friends. Swarming fans lined up outside awaiting her exit so that they could get her autograph. Two months later, Miley's co-stars on the tour, the Jonas Brothers—who have their own incredibly huge fan following—were in town to perform at the White House Easter Egg Roll. They dined at our Georgetown Morton's, also on a Sunday evening. The three brothers ordered the Chicago-style bone-in rib-eye and filets Mignon for their Easter feast, and were accompanied by twenty guests. ☙

ROASTED FINGERLING POTATOES

These tiny potatoes cook quickly spread out on a baking pan. They are crisp on the outside and gorgeously soft on the inside. It's not always easy to find fingerling potatoes (which are small, elongated tubers much favored by chefs), so you can substitute the smallest new potatoes you can find. **SERVES 6 TO 8**

2 tablespoons minced fresh rosemary

1½ teaspoons minced garlic

1 teaspoon sweet paprika

1 teaspoon salt

¼ teaspoon freshly ground black pepper

1 tablespoon Worcestershire sauce

¼ cup olive oil

2 pounds assorted fingerling potatoes or any baby-size red, Yukon Gold, or white potatoes

Preheat the oven to 375°F.

In a small bowl, mix together the rosemary, garlic, paprika, salt, and pepper.

In another small bowl, whisk together the Worcestershire sauce and oil.

Spread the potatoes in a baking dish and drizzle the Worcestershire sauce and oil mixture over the potatoes. Sprinkle the herb mixture evenly over the potatoes and toss to coat.

Roast for 35 to 40 minutes or until the potatoes are lightly browned, tender, and cooked through. Stir the potatoes several times during roasting. Serve immediately.

BLUE-CHEESE FRENCH FRIES

This is a recipe that we offer on our Bar 12*21 menu (the name stands for the day that we opened: December 21, 1978). Right now we have about fifty Bar 12*21s and are adding more every year. The bars are lively and spacious and a good way to introduce a new generation to our robust food and legendary service. The menu is mostly appetizers and some desserts: an elevated version of bar food. We had French fries on the menu and one day we added blue cheese—so decadent and so delicious. We suggest using frozen French fries here to make it easy, but if you prefer, by all means peel and cut up some all-purpose potatoes and deep-fry them. You may choose to do as we do and serve these as a first course, although they make a show-stopping side dish, too. Our guests love them; yours will, too! **SERVES 4**

5 tablespoons crumbled blue cheese

1½ tablespoons heavy cream

12 ounces good-quality, unseasoned, regular-cut frozen French fries

Seasoned salt

½ teaspoon minced fresh chives

Pinch of crushed red pepper flakes

Preheat the oven to 500°F or the temperature listed on the package of French fries.

In a small mixing bowl, mix about 3 tablespoons of the blue cheese with the cream until smooth and well blended. Spoon the mixture into a pastry bag fitted with a plain tip or into a small, sturdy plastic bag.

Cook the French fries according to package directions until golden brown. (Baking or frying is the best choice; do not microwave the fries.) Transfer the fries to a baking dish and season lightly with the seasoned salt.

Increase the oven temperature to 500°F, if necessary.

If using a plastic bag, push the cheese mixture into one corner and snip that corner from the bag. Gently squeeze the blue cheese over the fries in a spiral pattern, starting at the center of the dish and working outward. Sprinkle the remaining 2 tablespoons cheese evenly over the fries. Bake for about 1½ minutes until the cheese melts.

To serve, transfer the fries to a platter. Sprinkle with the chives and red pepper flakes. Serve immediately.

TWICE-BAKED POTATOES

These have become very popular at our parties in Morton's boardrooms—the name we use for our private dining rooms. The potatoes, filled with a sinfully delicious mixture of baked potato flesh, cream, sour cream, cheese, and eggs, are so good you barely need anything else for dinner. **SERVES 6**

6 large Idaho baking potatoes, each about 10 to 12 ounces

6 tablespoons (¾ stick) unsalted butter, at room temperature

¾ cup heavy cream

6 tablespoons sour cream

6 tablespoons minced fresh chives

6 ounces shredded Swiss cheese (1½ cups)

3 tablespoons freshly grated Parmesan cheese

3 large eggs, lightly beaten, at room temperature

1 tablespoon salt

½ tablespoon freshly ground black pepper

Preheat the oven to 400°F.

Pierce the potatoes a few times with a small, sharp knife. Bake the potatoes directly on the oven rack for about 1½ hours or until fork tender. Let the potatoes cool for about 15 minutes. Lower the oven temperature to 350°F.

Using a paring knife, cut an oval from the top of each potato. Scrape the flesh off the cut-out piece and put it in the bowl of an electric mixer fitted with the paddle attachment. Carefully scoop the flesh from the inside of the potatoes, leaving ½ inch of flesh, and put the scooped-out flesh in the bowl. Keep the potatoes' jackets intact.

Add the butter, cream, sour cream, chives, half of the Swiss cheese, the Parmesan cheese, eggs, salt, and pepper to the potato flesh in the bowl. Mix on high for about 30 seconds, or until well combined. Scrape down the sides of the bowl and mix for another 30 seconds. If you prefer, use a potato masher and large wooden spoon.

Spoon the potato mixture back into the jackets, mounding the mixture about ½ inch over the top. (Spoon any leftover potato mixture into a small casserole dish and bake alongside the potatoes.)

Transfer the potatoes to a large rimmed baking sheet or shallow roasting pan, sprinkle with the remaining Swiss cheese, and bake for 30 to 35 minutes or until the cheese melts and the potatoes are heated all the way through. Serve immediately.

MACARONI AND CHEESE

Talk about cheesy! If you like macaroni and cheese, this has it all, with four different cheeses and a little kick from the chile paste that says this is a very grown-up version of mac and cheese. Executive chef Chris Rook and I developed it at the request of Tom Baldwin, our chairman and CEO—who was right on target about what our guests like. It already happens to be a favorite of stand-up comedian/actor D. L. Hughley. **SERVES 6 TO 8**

12 ounces dried cavatappi or other small hollow, ridged pasta

1½ teaspoons unsalted butter, melted

¼ cup finely chopped yellow onion

1¼ cups heavy cream

6 ounces sharp cheddar cheese, shredded (about 2 cups), plus 5 ounces sharp cheddar cheese, coarsely shredded (about 1⅔ cups)

4 ounces cream cheese, cut into small cubes

3 ounces Parmesan cheese, freshly grated (about ⅔ cup)

1 ounce Swiss cheese, grated (about 6 tablespoons)

½ tablespoon chile paste, such as sambal oelek

Kosher salt

½ cup panko bread crumbs

Preheat the oven to 400°F.

Cook the pasta according to the package directions until al dente. Drain but leave a little water on the pasta to keep it moist. Reserve another ½ cup of pasta water to thin the sauce. Return the pasta to the cooking pot and cover to keep warm.

In a medium saucepan, melt the butter over medium heat and sauté the onion for about 1 minute or until tender. Add the cream and bring to a simmer. Stir in the 2 cups of shredded cheddar, the cream cheese, Parmesan, and Swiss cheese and cook, stirring, until the cheeses melt and are fully incorporated into the cream. Let the sauce reach a simmer and stir in the chile paste. You will have 2½ to 3 cups of sauce.

Remove from the heat and, using an immersion blender or handheld electric mixer, beat for about 45 seconds until the cheeses and onion are completely blended. The sauce will be thick; thin it with up to ½ cup of the reserved pasta water and mix well. Season to taste with salt.

Ladle the sauce over the pasta and mix well with a rubber spatula. Transfer to a deep 2-quart baking dish and spread the pasta and cheese evenly. Sprinkle the 1⅔ cups of coarsely shredded cheddar cheese over the casserole and sprinkle with the bread crumbs. Bake for 20 to 25 minutes or until hot and bubbling around the edges. Serve immediately.

HONEY-GLAZED APPLE PASTRY

DESSERTS

DOUBLE CHOCOLATE MOUSSE

—

STREUSEL CHEESECAKE

—

Armen Keteyian's Favorite
MRS. ARTINIAN'S CARROT CAKE

—

CRANBERRY-APPLE COBBLER

—

HONEY-GLAZED APPLE PASTRY

CRÈME BRÛLÉE

—

MORTON'S APPLE PIE COCKTAIL

—

TIRAMISU MORTINI

—

PISTACHIO MOCHATINI

DOUBLE CHOCOLATE MOUSSE

You might wonder what took us so long, but we only recently added chocolate mousse to our menu. Since then, restaurant guests have gone wild for it. We use Belgian bittersweet chocolate, which is of very high quality, but any good dark chocolate will do. If you are concerned about the uncooked egg whites called for here, use pasteurized egg whites, which are sold in cartons in supermarkets. This is rich and smooth and chocolaty. **SERVES 8**

1½ cups heavy cream

6 ounces semisweet or bittersweet dark
  chocolate, preferably Belgian, chopped into
  small pieces

1 tablespoon plus 1½ teaspoons unsweetened
  cocoa powder

½ cup egg whites (from 3 to 4 large eggs)
  or ½ cup pasteurized egg whites

⅛ teaspoon cream of tartar

⅛ teaspoon salt

¼ cup sugar

Whipped cream, for serving

In a saucepan, bring ¾ cup of the cream to a boil over medium-high heat.

Put the chocolate and cocoa in a heat-proof glass bowl and pour the hot cream over them. Let the mixture stand for about 1 minute and then whisk until blended. Be sure to break up any clumps of the cocoa. Set aside at room temperature for about 45 minutes, whisking occasionally to keep the mixture smooth. The chocolate needs to cool to 80°F.

In a chilled, dry bowl of an electric mixer fitted with the whisk attachment, beat the egg whites on high speed for 10 to 20 seconds or until they begin to foam. Add the cream of tartar and salt and beat for about 1 minute longer or until soft peaks form.

Sprinkle the sugar over the whites and continue to beat for 1 to 2 minutes longer or until the peaks are stiff but not dry. At this point, the mixer will make a "wop, wop, wop" sound.

Fold the whites into the cooled chocolate (make sure it's no warmer than 80°F before adding the whites).

Pour the remaining heavy cream into the bowl of the mixer and beat with the whisk attachment on high speed for about 2 minutes or until soft peaks form. Fold the whipped cream into the chocolate. Do not worry if a few flecks of whites remain in the chocolate.

Cover the bowl with plastic wrap and refrigerate for at least 4 hours or overnight. Serve the mousse spooned on dessert plates or in bowls. Top each serving with a little whipped cream. At Morton's we pipe the mousse into serving dishes using a pastry bag fitted with a star tip.

STREUSEL CHEESECAKE

This buttery and rich cake is not overly sweet, but sweet enough to please anyone who craves a cheesy dessert. Ours is not a typical cheesecake but is more like a cheese-filled coffee cake. In fact, it is wonderful for breakfast or brunch. If you want to dress it up, top the cake with canned fruit pie topping (also called "pie filling") such as blueberry or cherry after baking. If you do, refrigerate it for about an hour. It's delicious as it is, served without refrigerating. It also keeps well in the refrigerator for a day or so and freezes and travels well, too. **MAKES ONE 9-BY-13-INCH CAKE; SERVES 12 TO 14**

DOUGH

Vegetable oil cooking spray

3 cups all-purpose flour

1 cup sugar

1 teaspoon baking powder

1 teaspoon baking soda

1 cup (2 sticks) unsalted butter, cut into pieces

2 large eggs, lightly beaten

1 cup sour cream

1 teaspoon pure vanilla extract

FILLING

1 pound cream cheese, softened

1 cup sugar

1 large egg yolk

1 teaspoon pure vanilla extract

TOPPING

¼ cup all-purpose flour

¼ cup sugar

3 tablespoons cold unsalted butter

Preheat the oven to 375°F. Spray a 9 by 13 by 2-inch baking pan with vegetable spray.

To make the dough: In the bowl of a food processor fitted with the metal blade, pulse the flour, sugar, baking powder, and baking soda several times. Add the butter and pulse a few times until the butter is worked into the flour mixture and it resembles coarse crumbs. Turn the dough into a large mixing bowl.

Add the eggs, sour cream, and vanilla to the bowl and using a large spoon or rubber spatula, mix well until blended.

Spread half the dough into the baking pan, then pat evenly onto the bottom and push it into the corners and up the sides. It will come about 1 inch up the sides.

To make the filling: In the bowl of an electric mixer fitted with the paddle attachment, beat the cream cheese on medium speed for about 3 minutes until fluffy.

Add the sugar, egg yolk, and vanilla and beat for 1 to 2 minutes longer or until light and fluffy.

Dollop the filling at even intervals over the dough and then spread it evenly. Spread the remaining dough over the filling, working gently to cover the filling as evenly as you can. Be careful not to push the dough into the filling.

To make the topping: In a small bowl, stir together the flour and sugar. Add the butter a tablespoon at a time, and work it with a pastry blender, fork, or your fingers until it resembles coarse crumbs. Alternatively, you could make the topping in a food processor fitted with a metal blade. Pulse it 5 to 6 times to mix. Sprinkle the topping evenly over the top of the cheesecake.

Bake the cheesecake for 40 to 45 minutes, or until the top is slightly puffed and golden and the sides begin to pull away from the sides of the pan.

Let the cheesecake cool in the pan set on a wire rack. When cool, cut into squares to serve.

SPRINGTIME DINNER MENU

MRS. ARTINIAN'S CARROT CAKE

This has quickly become the favorite dessert of our favorite investigative reporter, Armen Keteyian. Armen is a great friend of Morton's and annually acts as the master of ceremonies for Morton's March of Dimes Legends Event in our Stamford, Connecticut restaurant. When we were looking for a great carrot cake, our vice president of operations, Chris Artinian, shared this recipe, which comes from of his mother, Marianne Artinian. **MAKES ONE 9-INCH LAYER CAKE; SERVES 12 TO 14**

CAKE

2 tablespoons unsalted butter, plus more
    for the pan
2 cups all-purpose flour, plus more for the pan
2 teaspoons baking soda
2 teaspoons ground cinnamon
½ teaspoon salt
4 large eggs
2 cups sugar
¾ cup vegetable oil
¾ cup buttermilk
2 teaspoons vanilla extract
⅓ cup crushed pineapple, drained
2 cups carrots, peeled and coarsely grated
1⅓ cups loosely packed shredded, sweetened
    coconut
2 cups finely chopped walnuts

BUTTERMILK GLAZE

1 cup sugar
½ cup buttermilk
8 tablespoons (1 stick) unsalted butter
1 tablespoon light corn syrup
½ teaspoon baking soda
1 tablespoon pure vanilla extract

FROSTING

1½ cups (3 sticks) unsalted butter, at room
    temperature
12 ounces cream cheese, at room temperature
3 cups confectioners' sugar
1½ teaspoons grated orange zest
1½ teaspoons fresh orange juice
1½ teaspoons pure vanilla extract

To make the cake: Preheat the oven to 350°F. Generously butter two 9-inch round cake pans, each about 1½ inches deep. Dust each cake pan with about 1 tablespoon of flour.

In a mixing bowl, sift together the flour, baking soda, cinnamon, and salt. In a large mixing bowl, whisk the eggs until blended. Add the sugar, oil, buttermilk, and vanilla and mix well.

recipe continues on next page

Add the pineapple, carrots, coconut, and 1 cup of the walnuts and mix well. Add the flour mixture and fold into the batter with a rubber spatula.

Divide the batter evenly between the cake pans. Bake on the center rack of the oven for about 40 minutes, or until the sides of the cakes pull away from the sides of the pans and a toothpick inserted in the center of the cake comes out clean.

Meanwhile, make the glaze: In a small saucepan, mix together the sugar, buttermilk, butter, corn syrup, and baking soda until well blended. Set the pan over medium heat and bring to a simmer. Cook for about 3 minutes, stirring, until heated through and the sugar dissolves.

Remove the pan from the heat and whisk in the vanilla. Set aside, covered, to keep warm.

Remove the cakes from the oven and put them, still in the pans, on wire racks sitting on baking sheets. Using a toothpick, poke about 20 holes in the top crust of each cake layer. Do not go any further than halfway through the cakes.

Whisk the glaze and pour it evenly over the cake layers. Let the cakes cool completely and then cover them, still in the pans, with plastic wrap and refrigerate for at least 2 hours and up to 8 hours, until completely chilled.

To make the frosting: In the bowl of an electric mixer fitted with the paddle attachment and set on medium speed, beat the butter and cream cheese for about 2 minutes or until fluffy.

Add the confectioners' sugar, orange zest, orange juice, and vanilla. Mix slowly so that the sugar doesn't fly out of the bowl. Gradually increase the speed and beat for about 1 minute or until the frosting is smooth.

To assemble: Remove the cake layers from the refrigerator and invert them on a work surface. You might need to run a kitchen knife around the edges to loosen the layers. Put 1 layer on a platter, glazed side down.

Put about 1½ cups (a third) of the frosting on the center of the cake layer and, using a spatula, spread it evenly over the cake. There should be a layer of frosting about ½ inch thick. If the frosting is soft, return the cake to the refrigerator to stiffen it up.

Put the other layer on top of the cake, glazed side down, and frost the top of the cake with about 1½ cups (a third) of the frosting.

With the remainder of the frosting, cover the sides of the cakes with a thin layer.

With the tip of the spatula, press lightly into the top layer of frosting and pull it up to form little spikes. Repeat over the entire top of the cake.

ᔥ CELEBRITY CLIP ᔥ

SOME OF THE world's most famous comedians give their own rave reviews of our Morton's steakhouses. The creative geniuses behind the successful comedy sitcom *Everybody Loves Raymond*, Phil Rosenthal, executive producer, and Ray Romano, the show's star, both dine regularly in our downtown Los Angeles Morton's. Stand-up comedian Rita Rudner finished her show's first run in Las Vegas with a celebratory meal at our Morton's just off the strip with her cast of thirty. Motion picture funnyman Jack Black was recently seen at our Morton's in Hackensack, New Jersey, and was so gracious when one of his leading fans (a four-year-old boy) asked for an autograph. After telling the boy a few jokes, he had a bunch of photos taken with his new young pal. And finally, talk show maven Ellen DeGeneres often dines at our Burbank, California, Morton's with her writers and producers. The restaurant is close to the studio and during one show, Ellen sent her renowned *Riff-Raff Room* guests to Morton's, where our staff arranged for a surprise birthday cake for the show's guest, actress Jenny McCarthy. ᔥ

Lightly sprinkle the top of the cake with about 3 tablespoons of chopped walnuts. Press the rest of the walnuts onto the sides of the cake. Make this a thicker layer than the nuts on top of the cake. Serve at room temperature.

CRANBERRY-APPLE COBBLER

Our director of new restaurant openings, Melanie McShane, makes this for the staff and training team every time we open a new Morton's The Steakhouse. Everyone loves it and has come to expect it. What would an opening be without Mel's cobbler, with luscious fruit topped with a rich, buttery cake? We had to include it in our book. **SERVES 12**

2½ pounds tart apples, such as Granny Smith (5 to 7 apples, depending on size), peeled, cored, and thinly sliced (about 8 cups)

1 cup dried cranberries (about 5 ounces)

¾ cup chopped walnuts

½ cup lightly packed dark brown sugar

1½ tablespoons dark rum

4 large eggs

1½ cups granulated sugar

2 cups all-purpose flour

1½ cups (3 sticks) unsalted butter, melted

½ tablespoon pure vanilla extract

Premium vanilla ice cream, for serving

Preheat the oven to 350°F. Grease a 9 by 13 by 2-inch baking pan with flavorless vegetable spray or shortening.

In a large mixing bowl, toss the apples with the cranberries, walnuts, brown sugar, and rum. Spread the mixture in the baking pan.

In the bowl of an electric mixer fitted with the paddle attachment, beat the eggs on medium speed for about 2 minutes or until lightened in color. Add the granulated sugar and beat for about 2 minutes or until smooth. With the mixer on low speed, beat in the flour and melted butter, alternating them and beginning and ending with the flour. When combined, stir in the vanilla.

Slowly pour the batter over the fruit until it is completely covered. Allow the batter to settle around the fruit gently; you might have to move a few apple slices to let the batter "settle in" completely. Bake for 45 minutes to 1 hour or until the topping is evenly golden brown. Serve warm or at room temperature with vanilla ice cream.

HONEY-GLAZED APPLE PASTRY

One of my favorite cooking partners is John Bettin, the former president of Morton's The Steakhouse. He's a good cook and even better company, and I was thrilled when he taught me how to make these splendid galettes. Says John: "Many years ago I was involved with a small seafood restaurant chain that specialized in mesquite-grilled fresh fish. We were looking for a simple yet elegant dessert to complement a great seafood meal and my good friend and mentor, Alan Lamoureux, came up with this recipe. I have re-created it from memory and it still conjures up warm memories from those days." I love this dessert: It's very simple and has great visual appeal as well as great flavors. **SERVES 8**

One 17.3-ounce package puff pastry sheets, frozen

2 to 3 tablespoons all-purpose flour

1½ pounds Granny Smith apples (about 3 apples), cored, peeled, and thinly sliced, see Note

4 teaspoons sugar

3 tablespoons honey

8 scoops premium vanilla ice cream

Remove both pastry sheets from the carton and thaw at room temperature for 30 to 45 minutes.

Preheat the oven to 425°F. Line two 12 by 18-inch sheet pans with parchment paper.

On a lightly floured surface, unfold the thawed pastry sheets and dust the tops lightly with flour. Using a rolling pin, roll each sheet into a 13-inch square, large enough so that each yields four 6-inch rounds.

Using a paper template or a bowl that measures 6 inches across, cut the rounds from the pastry sheets. You will have 8 rounds. Dust off any excess flour and lay the rounds on the baking sheets, 4 to a sheet. Make sure they do not touch each other.

Using the center of each pastry round as an axis, fan the larger apple slices in a circle on top of the pastry round, overlapping them slightly. Cover each pastry round completely. If necessary, use the smaller apple slices to fill in any large gaps. Sprinkle the apple slices with the sugar, distributing it evenly.

Bake for 16 to 20 minutes, or until the puff pastry is golden and the apples are tender and their edges lightly browned.

Meanwhile, in a small saucepan, warm the honey over medium-low heat just until warm and thin enough to brush easily.

Transfer an apple tart to each of 8 dessert plates. Brush each tart with warm honey and top with a small scoop of vanilla ice cream.

NOTE: If you have a mandoline, use it to slice the apples as thin as you can. You can cut the apples before rolling and cutting the pastry; put the thin slices in a large bowl filled with cold water into which you have squeezed the juice of ½ lemon. This will keep the apple slices from turning brown.

The dessert can be prepared several hours ahead of time. Bake the tarts and hold them at room temperature until ready to serve. Do not drizzle with honey until reheating. Just before serving, preheat the oven to 400°F and warm the apple tarts on parchment-paper-lined baking sheets for 5 to 10 minutes. Brush with warm honey and serve with ice cream.

✎ CELEBRITY CLIP ✎

MORTON'S THE STEAKHOUSE has a rich thirty-year history of giving back to the communities that support us, and very often celebrities have generously given their time and energy to help us achieve success. Over our thirty years, we've raised approximately thirteen million dollars for large and small not-for-profit organizations, including the Crohn's and Colitis Foundation of America; Meals on Wheels Association of America; the American Red Cross; the Illinois Restaurant Association's ProStart Foundation, a scholarship program for aspiring culinary and hospitality students; and Hogar Cuna San Cristóbal, an organization that works with children and youth in Puerto Rico.

For ten years, we've hosted an annual Legends Event at our Stamford, Connecticut, restaurant, which featured top sports celebrities such as Phil Simms, Bill Belichick, Keith Hernandez, Willie Randolph, and broadcaster Hannah Storm. Those events alone cumulatively raised more than $700,000 for the March of Dimes Southern Connecticut Division. To celebrate thirty years as America's leading steakhouse, Morton's has partnered with the Make-A-Wish Foundation for a national "30 Wishes for 30 Years" campaign, through which we expect to raise significant funds for children with life-threatening illnesses. ✎

CRÈME BRÛLÉE

This dessert is made with cream and egg yolks and is wickedly delicious. Our guests order it with great pleasure and frequency. Crème brûlée originated in Europe but is so popular in North America that I am not sure anyone thinks of it as French or Swiss anymore. Instead, they think of it as a reason to smile with happy anticipation! I urge you to use a vanilla bean for this. They are easy to use and make a big difference when it comes to flavor. If you cannot, substitute 1½ teaspoons of pure vanilla extract. **SERVES 6**

CRÈME BRÛLÉE

1 cup sugar

12 large egg yolks, lightly beaten

2 cups heavy cream

2 cups whole milk

½ vanilla bean, split open

GARNISH

6 tablespoons sugar

6 sprigs of fresh mint

18 raspberries

Preheat the oven to 300°F. Position a rack in the center of the oven.

In a mixing bowl, whisk together the sugar and egg yolks just until the egg yolks moisten the sugar.

In a saucepan, combine the cream and milk. Add the vanilla bean and heat over medium heat for 5 to 6 minutes or until bubbles appear around the edges and a thermometer lowered into the liquid registers about 110°F. Lift the bean from the pan and, with a small, sharp knife, scrape the vanilla seeds into the saucepan. Discard the bean.

Pour a little of the hot milk mixture into the egg yolks to temper them, whisking constantly to prevent the eggs from curdling and to disperse the vanilla seeds evenly. Pour the tempered yolks and sugar back into the saucepan, whisking constantly over very low heat for 1 to 2 minutes or until heated through and the sugar melts. Do not cook any longer; the custard cooks fully in the oven.

Set six 8-ounce crème brûlée dishes or ramekins in a roasting pan large enough to hold them without touching (you may have to use 2 pans). Ladle the custard into the ramekins nearly to the rims.

Carefully transfer the pan to the oven rack. Spoon a little more custard into the ramekins to use it all and top off the ramekins. Pour enough hot water into the roasting pan to come

recipe continues on next page

about three quarters of the way up the sides of the ramekins. Take care when adding the water so it does not splash into the custard.

Bake for about 55 minutes or until the custard is firm around the edges and jiggles a little in the center and the top is set and lightly colored.

Remove the pan from the oven and let the custards cool in the water for about 30 minutes or until you can comfortably lift them from the water. Set the ramekins on the counter to cool for 30 minutes longer. Cover each ramekin with plastic wrap and refrigerate for at least 6 hours and up to 24 hours.

Shortly before serving, remove the brûlées from the refrigerator. Sprinkle 1 tablespoon of sugar evenly over each one.

Run a small kitchen torch over the sugar to melt, brown, and crisp it. This will take about 1½ minutes for each ramekin. Let the ramekins sit for about 2 minutes to give the sugar time to harden. Alternatively, slide the ramekins under the broiler about 2 inches from the heat source for about 2 minutes to brown the sugar.

Garnish each brûlée with a mint leaf and 3 raspberries and serve.

MORTON'S APPLE PIE COCKTAIL

For a mellow, richly flavored cocktail, try this dessert drink. The heady flavors of apple pie play on your tongue for a thoroughly satisfying sweet treat. **SERVES 1**

1 ounce apple schnapps

1 tablespoon golden raisins

1 tablespoon brown sugar

½ ounce Goldschlager Liqueur

1 ounce dark crème de cacao

2 tablespoons apple juice

2 tablespoons heavy cream

Ground cinnamon, for garnish

Put the apple schnapps, raisins, brown sugar, and Goldschlager in a cocktail shaker and with the back of a long-handled spoon or a cocktail muddler, press on the sugar and raisins until the sugar dissolves and the raisins are lightly mashed.

Add the crème de cacao, apple juice, and cream. Fill the shaker with ice cubes and shake 15 times. Strain into a martini glass and garnish with a sprinkling of cinnamon.

TIRAMISU MORTINI

You won't need to serve dessert when you offer this tiramisu in a glass—with a punch! The brandy, cream, and liqueurs come together for a rich, smooth, gloriously indulgent dessert cocktail. **SERVES 1**

1 ounce brandy

2 tablespoons heavy cream

½ ounce coffee liqueur, such as Starbucks or Kahlúa

½ ounce dark crème de cacao

1 large egg yolk

1 teaspoon mascarpone cheese

Pure maple syrup

Semisweet chocolate shavings

Pour the brandy, cream, liqueur, crème de cacao, egg yolk, and mascarpone in a cocktail shaker. Add a drop of maple syrup and shake 15 times.

Pour into a martini glass and garnish with freshly grated chocolate shavings.

PISTACHIO MOCHATINI

This sweet cocktail ends any meal in style. Be sure the pistachios are unsalted and thoroughly crushed for full effect.

SERVES 1

2 tablespoons Hershey's shell syrup

3 tablespoons crushed, unsalted pistachio nuts

1 orange slice

1 ounce rum, see Note

1 ounce coffee liqueur, such as Starbucks or Kahlúa

2 tablespoons heavy cream

2 tablespoons Baristella pistachio syrup

Chill a martini glass in the refrigerator for about 1 hour or until very cold. Pour the syrup into the glass and rotate it on an angle so that the syrup spreads up the glass about a third of the way. It will harden on the cold glass.

Spread the nuts in a shallow dish. Moisten the rim of the glass with the orange slice and then press the rim of the glass in the nuts. They will adhere to the juice.

Pour the rum, liqueur, cream, and syrup in a cocktail shaker filled with ice. Shake 15 times and then pour into the martini glass.

NOTE: We use Cruzan Estate Diamond rum, which is a relatively light rum and good for mixing with other ingredients.

Sauces, Dressings, and Basics

Dijon Vinaigrette

—

Tuscan Bread Crumbs

—

Thai Cream Sauce

—

Clarified Butter

—

Au Jus

—

Beurre Blanc

DIJON VINAIGRETTE

You might be surprised to see the salad dressing mix in this recipe, but take our word for it: It works! Try this with any salad made with leafy greens. **MAKES ABOUT 2½ CUPS**

⅔ cup white balsamic vinegar

½ cup Dijon mustard

3½ tablespoons Italian salad dressing mix, such as Good Seasons, see Note

1 cup extra-virgin olive oil

In a medium mixing bowl, combine the vinegar and ⅓ cup water. Whisk in the mustard and salad dressing mix until well mixed. Add the olive oil and whisk until the dressing is emulsified.

Let the dressing rest for a few minutes before using so that the flavors can blend. Refrigerate in a tightly lidded glass or rigid plastic container for up to 7 days and whisk before using.

NOTE: If you use Good Seasons brand mix, 2 packets work well.

TUSCAN BREAD CRUMBS

We depend on these nicely flavored bread crumbs for our Tuscan Pork Chops on page 154 and Chef Chris Rook's Sword-fish on page 175. They add depth and interest to a number of dishes, and they are easy to make. They keep for about a month. **MAKES ABOUT 1 ½ CUPS**

2 to 3 slices thick-cut white bread
   (4 to 5 ounces), crusts removed
½ cup freshly grated Parmesan cheese

1¾ teaspoons garlic powder
¾ teaspoon freshly ground white pepper

Tear the bread into pieces and put in the bowl of a food processor fitted with the metal blade. Pulse until the bread is ground into fine crumbs. You will have about 1 cup of crumbs.

Transfer the crumbs to a small mixing bowl. Add the Parmesan, garlic powder, and pepper, mix well, and use immediately or refrigerate in an airtight container for up to 3 days. You can also freeze the crumbs for up to 1 month.

THAI CREAM SAUCE

Few sauces taste better than this one when you want something bright and zesty. And few are easier to make. We love it with tuna and serve it with our Tuna Sashimi Burgers on page 43 and our Tuna Canapés on page 48. **MAKES ABOUT ½ CUP**

½ tablespoon Thai chile paste   **½ cup store-bought ranch dressing**

In a small mixing bowl, stir the chile paste into the dressing until smooth. Strain through a fine-mesh sieve into another container, cover, and refrigerate until needed. The dressing will keep for up to 1 week.

CLARIFIED BUTTER

Clarified butter can be heated to higher temperatures than other butter, which is why we use it so often. It's not hard to make. When refrigerated, it solidifies and turns a little grainy, but it melts easily and becomes liquid again. **MAKES ABOUT 1¼ CUPS**

1½ cups (3 sticks) unsalted butter

In a small saucepan over medium heat, cook the butter for about 5 minutes, or until completely melted and simmering gently.

Remove from the heat and let stand at room temperature for about 10 minutes, or until the solids settle on the bottom of the pan. Skim the foam off the top and discard.

Carefully pour or ladle the clear liquid clarified butter into a storage container and leave the milk solids in the pan. Discard the solids. Let the butter cool and then refrigerate the clarified butter for up to 1 week.

AU JUS

We always spoon a little au jus over steaks before serving. You may decide to forego this step, relying instead on the natural juices in the meat, but if you make this sauce, your steaks will have just a little more flavor and a little more flair. It keeps in the refrigerator for a few days, so you can make it ahead of time. **MAKES ABOUT 1 GENEROUS CUP**

1 cup reconstituted store-bought veal demi-glace, see Note, page 117

2½ teaspoons commercial beef base, see Note, page 81

1¼ teaspoons commercial chicken base, see Note, page 81

½ teaspoon whole black peppercorns

⅛ teaspoon garlic powder

⅛ teaspoon dried thyme

1 bay leaf

Pinch of freshly ground white pepper

In a medium saucepan, combine 1¼ cups water with the demi-glace, beef base, chicken base, peppercorns, garlic powder, thyme, bay leaf, and white pepper. Whisk well. Bring to a boil over medium-high heat and cook at a boil, uncovered, whisking occasionally, for about 25 minutes, or until glossy and smooth.

Strain through a chinois or fine-mesh sieve into a metal bowl. Discard the solids. Let cool, then cover and refrigerate for at least 1 hour until chilled. Scrape off any fat that has congealed on the surface. Use right away or transfer to a lidded container and refrigerate for up to 3 days.

NOTE: If you decide to double or triple the amount of au jus you make at one time, cool the strained sauce in a bowl set in a larger one filled with ice cubes and water. This is the best way to cool large amounts of hot liquid. For the 1 cup we make here, it's not necessary.

BEURRE BLANC

This is a standard French-style cream sauce that is endlessly versatile. If you have an immersion blender, it's easier than ever. Take your time the first few times you make this until you get the hang of it and you will be rewarded with a smooth, satiny sauce with subtle but gorgeous flavor. We use it in our recipes for Baked Sea Scallops with Beurre Blanc, page 185, and Grilled Shrimp with Red Pepper Beurre Blanc, page 184. **MAKES ABOUT 2 CUPS**

1 teaspoon olive oil

1 large shallot, minced (about ¼ cup)

⅓ cup dry white wine

¾ cup heavy cream

12 tablespoons (1½ sticks) unsalted butter, softened

1 teaspoon fresh lemon juice

¼ teaspoon salt

Freshly ground white pepper

In a medium nonreactive saucepan, heat the olive oil over medium-low heat. Add the shallot and sauté for 2 to 3 minutes, or until it softens without coloring. Add the wine, raise the heat to medium-high, and bring to a boil. Reduce the heat and simmer for 3 to 4 minutes, or until the wine reduces and the liquid coats the bottom of the pan. Add the cream and simmer, stirring often, for 5 to 7 minutes, or until reduced by half.

Reduce the heat to low and begin adding the butter, a tablespoon at a time, whisking after each addition. Do not allow the cream to boil once the butter is added.

Remove the pan from the heat. Using a handheld immersion blender, beat for 5 to 10 seconds, or until smooth. Lift the beater and then immerse again and beat for a few seconds. Repeat this process to produce a silken sauce. If you do not have a handheld immersion blender, do this in an electric mixer or by hand. The immersion blender does the best job.

Add the lemon juice and salt and season to taste with white pepper. Stir to blend. Strain the sauce through a fine-mesh sieve or chinois into a small saucepan.

Keep the sauce warm over low heat, making sure the temperature remains between 110° to 120°F, for up to 1 hour or until ready to serve.

ACKNOWLEDGMENTS

Many people helped me with this book, and I could not have done it without them. Tylor Field III, our vice president of wine and spirits, is an expert and a joy to work with. Not only is his knowledge encyclopedic, but he is a kind and patient teacher who thinks long and hard about how food will taste with the wine or spirit, and vice versa.

Neither Tylor nor I could have written this book without the support of Allen J. Bernstein, our chairman emeritus, who spearheaded our successful first book, *Morton's Steak Bible,* and Tom Baldwin. Tom was named chairman, CEO, and president of Morton's Restaurant Group in December 2005 and since then has helped us broaden our appeal by evolving the menu and our overall brand, which in turn, has introduced many new guests to Morton's. Under Tom's leadership and with the guidance and support of the rest of the executive team, we are retrofitting our bars to be more relevant and attractive to the slightly younger generation, as well as to our loyal and longstanding guests. These Morton's bars have been named Bar 12•21, a tribute to the date Arnie Morton and I first opened Morton's on State Street in Chicago: December 21, 1978. We have updated many of our bars in existing restaurants, and outfit new restaurants with them upon opening. The bars are spacious, energetic, exciting places, perfect for unwinding after work or getting the weekend off to a good start, and offer a special Bar Bites menu. And, just as Tom and our management team predicted, they are drawing crowds that enjoy our cocktails and bar food as well as the spirit and liveliness of Bar 12•21.

I would like to thank Roger Drake, our chief communications officer, who wrote all the celebrity stories and was instrumental in getting this book from concept to reality.

I asked two of my favorite cooking partners and trusted friends to join me in my Chicago kitchen to "cook through" the more than 100 recipes found on these pages. Chris Rook is our executive chef and one of the finest chefs I know. Donna Rundle, our manager of restaurant services, is a longtime friend and skilled home cook. Both Chris and Donna are full of good cheer and have enormous patience and I thank them for helping me make this an enticing and appealing book. During long winter afternoons, we cooked all the dishes you will find here, improved upon them when necessary, and came up with new ideas when something didn't turn out perfectly. We had a great time. We learned a lot, laughed a lot, and ate a lot. We hope the recipes we chose, after some trial and error, will inspire you to do the same with your family and friends.

Tylor and I would like to thank our certified sommelier, Sara Fasolino, for her help with some of the wine, beer, and spirits pairings. She has a gifted palate.

I also want to thank Mary Goodbody, who put together the manuscript for us. She worked closely with Tylor, Chris, Donna, Roger and me to ensure that all our ideas were clearly realized and the information and recipes are accurate. Jane Dystel, our indefatigable agent, saw this project through from start to finish and offered support and welcome advice along the way. Debi Callan helped test the recipes so that they work perfectly in the home kitchen and Lisa Thornton helped with the manuscript.

Lastly, but certainly not least, I thank our skilled and patient editor, Rica Allannic, and her team at Clarkson Potter. Rica's support and belief in the book never wavered and it would not look as beautiful nor read as well without her generous, careful attention to it.

INDEX

Note: *Italicized* page numbers indicate photographs.

CONVERSION CHART
EQUIVALENT IMPERIAL AND METRIC MEASUREMENTS

American cooks use standard containers, the 8-ounce cup and a table-spoon that takes exactly 16 level fillings to fill that cup level. Measuring by a cup makes it very difficult to give weight equivalents, as a cup of densely packed butter will weigh considerably more than a cup of flour. The easiest way therefore to deal with cup measurements in recipes is to take the amount by volume rather than weight. Thus the equation reads:

1 cup = 240 ml = 8 fl. oz. ½ cup = 120 ml = 4 fl. oz.

In the States, butter is often measured in sticks. One stick is the equivalent of 8 tablespoons. One tablespoon of butter is therefore equivalent to ½ ounce/15 grams.

LIQUID MEASURES

Fluid Ounces	U.S.	Imperial	Milliliters
⅛	1 teaspoon	1 teaspoon	5
¼	2 teaspoons	1 dessertspoon	10
½	1 tablespoon	1 tablespoon	14
1	2 tablespoons	2 tablespoons	28
2	¼ cup	4 tablespoons	56
4	½ cup		120
5		¼ pint or 1 gill	140
6	¾ cup		170
8	1 cup		240
9			250, ¼ liter
10	1¼ cups	½ pint	280
12	1½ cups		340
15		¾ pint	420
16	2 cups		450
18	2¼ cups		500, ½ liter
20	2½ cups	1 pint	560
24	3 cups		675
25		1¼ pints	700
27	3½ cups		750
30	3¾ cups	1½ pints	840
32	4 cups or 1 quart		900
35		1¾ pints	980
36	4½ cups		1000, 1 liter
40	5 cups	2 pints or 1 quart	1120

SOLID MEASURES

U.S. AND IMPERIAL MEASURES		METRIC MEASURES	
Ounces	Pounds.	Grams	Kilos
1		28	
2		56	
3½		100	
4	¼	112	
5		140	
6		168	
8	½	225	
9		250	¼
12	¾	340	
16	1	450	
18		500	½
20	1¼	560	
24	1½	675	
27		750	¾
28	1¾	780	
32	2	900	
36	2¼	1000	1
40	2½	1100	
48	3	1350	
54		1500	1½

OVEN TEMPERATURE EQUIVALENTS

Fahrenheit	Celsius	Gas Mark	Description
225	110	¼	Cool
250	130	½	
275	140	1	Very Slow
300	150	2	
325	170	3	Slow
350	180	4	Moderate
375	190	5	
400	200	6	Moderately Hot
425	220	7	Fairly Hot
450	230	8	Hot
475	240	9	Very Hot
500	250	10	Extremely Hot

Any broiling recipes can be used with the grill of the oven, but beware of high-temperature grills.

EQUIVALENTS FOR INGREDIENTS

all-purpose flour—plain flour
baking sheet—oven tray
buttermilk—ordinary milk
cheesecloth—muslin
coarse salt—kitchen salt
cornstarch—cornflour
eggplant—aubergine

granulated sugar—castor sugar
half and half—12% fat milk
heavy cream—double cream
light cream—single cream
lima beans—broad beans
parchment paper—greaseproof paper
plastic wrap—cling film

scallion—spring onion
shortening—white fat
unbleached flour—strong, white flour
vanilla beans—vanilla pod
zest—rind
zucchini—courgettes or marrow